Stories from
Under the Wing

Lee Kalnin

Copyright © 2020 by **Lee Kalnin**

All rights reserved. No part of this publication may be reproduced, distributed or transmitted in any form or by any means, without prior written permission.

Weaver of Words Publisher
1056 Mallard Place
Qualicum Beach, B.C., Canada V9K 1E8
www.wordweaver.info

Under the Wing/Lee Kalnin -- 1st ed.
ISBN 978-0-9937449-9-0

For my darling Phil,
who said there will be no sadness ~
I want to hear laughter.
He did not look for a way out.
He walked forward as he walked toward all things ~
with courage and incredible strength.

and for my wonderful and wise
granddaughter Rees

And then he was gone.
What's left behind?
All that remains, in the end, is love.
The love he had for us.
The love we still have for him.
And true love never dies.

—*The Reason You Walk* by Wab Kinew

Contents

PART I: PHIL

Diagnosis	1
Phil Started Out as a Child	7
Selecting the Right Day	15
An Elegy of Words	23
Can I Ever Be Happy?	29
Our First School Together	35
Under the Wing	37
Texada Tradition	43
You Can't Do That Here!	51
Mr. Kanasawa	57
Kick It Up a Notch	59
A Tale of Two Braces	63
Jumping Curb	67
Two Rings	69
The Stone	75
Passion for Flight	79
Dreaded Meeting	85
Eagle	91
To Live is to Lose	93
A Fine Friendship Flowers	97
Pat's Love	101
The Lives Phil Touched	103
Private Museum	107

PART II: LEE

Running Away 111
Cry Yourself to Sleep, Little One 117
Hidden Deep 121
Ten Easy Pieces 127
Goodie Two Shoes 133
Babies 139
I am Determined to Have a Wholesome Lifestyle 143
Near-Death Experience 147
Protector 153
Allergy 159
Locomotive Love 165
I Don't WANT to Quit 171
But, Can I Do It? 177
Finding Lost Stones 185
First Flight to the USA 191
Little Brown Bear 197
Nana Mac's Air 201
She Does Only Fabulous 205
The Dog Ate My Homework 209
Blood Brother 213
Once There Was 221
My Most Recent Trip Around the Sun 227
Hands 233

Part I

PHIL

CHAPTER ONE

Diagnosis

Phil's diagnosis changes our lives from beautiful bright ivory to dark ebony.

We walk slowly out of the building, heavily, as though we are in boots slogging through mud. But it is not muddy, and we are not wearing boots. It is a beautiful September day.

All I can think about is this diagnosis. The simple act of opening the truck door, of climbing up into the seat, is difficult for me. Once inside, Phil and I sit close together. His strong arm rests against mine. I feel the security of the hair on his arm brush mine.

We don't look in one another's eyes. Intense pain brims there. But it is not spilling over. It is too horrendous for that. We don't talk. We are stunned and staring and paralyzed. They have shot poisoned arrows of terror through us.

Crashing, crashing, our world has imploded. We don't move for a long time, remaining still like statues. We don't notice this day is coming to a close, and the world carries on without us. Orange and yellow, the sun begins its descent.

Neither do we remember we have a long drive home. It seems we are not really breathing. We are stuck in this unmoving place of fear, just we two, alone ~ here outside the Victoria Cancer Agency.

~~~~~~~

A beautiful young oncologist in a short skirt and high heels enters her office. We occupy the only two chairs. The only other seat is a tiny step stool. Without hesitation, she draws it up for herself. It is an unseemly position, there below us, for one so competent and accomplished. But she is not there to impress, and I sense she would rather be anywhere else but here at this moment.

Her concerned look curdles my blood.

Phil has endured test after test this morning, and she has come to give us the results.

She does not wait, but says gently, "Phil, you have cancer. It's called mesothelioma, and it's asbestos-related cancer. Have you ever worked with asbestos?"

"Only for forty years," Phil says.

Though she is tender, the news is bad.

"There is nothing we can do for you, Phil. We can only buy you a little time, perhaps ten months."

The news devastates us.

~~~~~~~

We travel home to meet a new oncologist and begin chemotherapy.

Life, as we know it, so filled with laughter and fun and nearly completely untroubled, changes immediately. Now every thought, every plan, every detail of every day of our lives is focused entirely on keeping Phil alive.

Phil remains optimistic and determined. He rejects sadness, wants laughter. He remains positive, which is his way, every day. Because of him, I remain optimistic, too.

He becomes good friends with his second female oncologist. He has a talent for picking his doctors ~ young and beautiful. His many nurses adore him because of his never-ending sense of humour.

To stay sane during treatments, some of which last eight hours, we work through books and books of crossword puzzles, as the poison drips unrelentingly into his vein.

Drip. Drip. Drip.

I sit opposite him, pencilling letters upside down in the little boxes. It occupies his mind. It occupies my mind. It is not a pretty place to be. There are a lot of sick people in this room. Twelve big chairs of sick people, all with IV's and each of them trying to stay strong.

Phil is sick, very sick. There are times when his blood counts are not even high enough for treatment, and we are turned away, always to his great disappointment, for he is determined to live and believes chemotherapy is the way.

For over two years, Phil endures the ravages of chemotherapy. He becomes sicker. He becomes thinner.

Chemotherapy continues relentlessly. Some days are bad, and then there are the days that are much worse.

Then we have the second-worst day of our lives so far. The chemotherapy is withdrawn because it is not working.

Our doctor, who has become our friend since he comes to our home almost every day to check on Phil, recognizes our optimistic outlook and one day says, "Phil, I must be very clear. This terrible disease IS going to take your life."

He describes the process. "First, you will stop eating. Then you will stop drinking."

Because of Phil's wish to die at home, the doctor brings documents for Phil and me to sign.

I nurse Phil. I want to nurse Phil. I choose to nurse Phil. I want to do everything I can for him. There are so many procedures the nurses carry out. I ask if they would train me to do some of them, and they do. I think they are grateful. I have an abundant supply of the equipment they will need, and I lay it out every day, in the order they will need it, ahead of their arrival. These extraordinary and caring nurses are with us constantly.

Then the day comes when the nurse cannot get Phil's pain under control. She phones his doctor repeatedly for instructions on the administration of the morphine.

Phil has been weeks in a hospital bed beside our own bed just inches away so that I will be right beside him. On this very difficult day, I sit on our bed watching him and think that at last, the nurse was successful and has his pain under control. His breathing becomes softer at last. He breathes in. He breathes out ~ softly. He breathes in. He breathes out.

~~~~~~~

He does not breathe in.

At this exact same instant as Phil does not breathe in, this very same second, on this hot July day, his doctor calls out from the screen door, "Hello, can I come in?"

I run to him, uttering the unthinkable.

"I think he is gone ~ just now."

How can the doctor, our friend, be arriving at such an urgent time?

He knows the way well and goes quickly to Phil's side. He presses a finger to his carotid.

He gently says, "I am so sorry, Lee."

He holds me briefly, but I need to have my arms around Phil.

I heave with sobs and cry, "No, no, NO."

I hold Phil's hands, both in mine. I kiss his face. I cry his name.

Our doctor says, "Who shall I call? I will call anyone you like."

He calls my next-door neighbours, Margret and Jean-Marc, who run over in their bare feet. He calls Michelle, my daughter. He calls the funeral home.

I stay with Phil.

Everyone arrives.

~~~~~~~

I am failing to acknowledge the reality of Phil's death fully. It is an epic quest involving ultimate failure.

The pain of loss is so intense, so severe, so constant, so relentless. Sometimes, I feel I can barely survive.

I evade the pain, encounter it, evade it, then encounter it again, for it is unendurable, all at once.

I constantly remember the eighteen wonderful years we had together ~ times of great laughter, great joy, and great love.

CHAPTER TWO

Phil Started Out as a Child

Who's the funniest person YOU know? Funny people are the best kind, aren't they? Living with a funny person can make life hilarious. Hilarious EVERY day of your life.

Phil proves his hilarity.

Phil started out as a child and says he can remember his actual birth.

He says earnestly, "I remember every moment of my birth. There I am, relaxing in a dark cozy wet place, minding my own business when I am surprised to find myself in a brightly lit room with doctors all around. Then one of them slaps me, and I don't even know what I've done."

I want this little boy self to grow to be a man, but not yet, Phil. You have a lot of life to experience first.

Phil is a big idea, a man everyone loves, a man who makes everyone laugh, a laugh a minute ~ six feet, heavily built, confident but modest.

Phil helps me with all the chores.

He says, "There are no pink and blue jobs. I don't really vacuum. I just knock the lumps off."

He says, "We should ALL live life on the edge. If we don't, we are taking up too much space."

~~~~~~~

But let's start at the beginning.

When he is six years old, Phil tells his brothers, "Come! Come and watch me fly. I'm going to really fly."

He makes the cardboard wings himself. He tapes them carefully to his skinny little brown arms. In the intense heat of this Manitoba summer, he trudges up to the six-foot rock cliffs where they play. The rocks are smooth, not jagged. His brothers crowd around him.

"Watch me now. Watch me!"

He takes a deep breath and jumps off, holding his thin arms wearing the cardboard wings out from his sides at right angles. He REALLY wants to fly. He KNOWS he can fly. He TRIES his best. But, despite his great hope and desire, he rockets down and lands in a crumple.

He is the second youngest of four boys. He and the older two brothers form The Three Musketeers and find ways to get into lots of trouble. They grow up in an isolated village that provides endless days of adventure. After their oatmeal and brown sugar breakfast, they leave and are gone for the entire day. They are not expected home at all until dinnertime.

These skinny young brown boys take turns stealing a few matches so they can make a little campfire up against the rocks of their playground. They pick their own lunch. In the wild, there are good things to eat. Together, they harvest blueberries, Saskatoon berries, and wild strawberries. Chins drip with colourful blue and red juice. Desserts are wild hazelnuts.

Jim says, "Chuck, you're in charge of peeling the birch bark for tea."

The old can with a wire handle had a label that read "Marvel Early June Peas" before it was scorched off.

Keep on growing up, little Phil, but there are still more experiences.

~~~~~~~

Two glorious months are free from school. They spend happy entire summers at a neighbouring farm. The boys don't return home until September. As the sun rises each already-hot morning, they slog with pails and pitchforks for the daily chores.

At the end of the day, though, they are rewarded for their sweaty work with bareback rides on the dusty wide backs of the draft horses, brown bony little legs sticking not down, but straight out on these broad backs as they bounce along.

These huge horses love their freedom. At the end of this long day, they are happy to be out of their harnesses and tack and not straining with work. They pay no mind to their young riders and go wherever they want to go, which is likely back to the barn for forkfuls of hay and a pail of crunchy oats.

Family fodder comes from the lush kitchen gardens, from chickens, eggs, and venison. A favourite is home-smoked goldeye fish from the Winnipeg River.

~~~~~~~

Today little Phil is mad at his oldest brother and is seeking revenge. Quietly, quietly, he takes an egg from the icebox. Stealthily, he climbs high up on the wooden boxes that are stacked behind the back door. At the top, he can see and, more importantly, he can reach right over. He waits patiently. He waits, and he waits, and he waits until the right brother comes through the door.

Now, at last, here he comes! He lifts the egg as high as his small arms can go, he arches over backward, and he strikes. He brings his stolen raw egg down like lightning to smash it with glee on the top of his brother's head.

With rivers of yolk running through his hair and down into his eyes, Jim cries, "Mom! Mom!"

Phil smiles. His revenge is sweet. He doesn't even mind having to pay the five cents to his mother for the egg.

~~~~~~~

As with a lot of the local families, money is short, so Phil is thrilled when he receives the gift of an old metal wagon. The little Radio Flyer is so worn out there is no red left. It is a solid rust-brown colour. No rubber remains on the metal wheels, so its constant squeaking alerts everyone to Phil's whereabouts. He loves his treasure so much he drags it with him everywhere he goes ~ down the gravel roads and over the big rocks, rattling and screeching.

Grow up, little Phil, but there are more and more adventures waiting for you yet.

~~~~~~~

For years all he asked for at Christmas was a rifle. Finally, under the tree is a beautiful plastic rifle. When his baby brother wants it, Phil is not about to share. His mother, in a fury, hits him with it and smashes it to smithereens.

And so, Phil makes his own rifles now, with wood and pipe and little tins of brown stain. These realistic-looking toy rifles bring kids from miles around begging to be allowed to play with them.

~~~~~~~

Some of Phil's adventures are, well, difficult.

One day the white gossamer curtains are billowing through the open kitchen window, and Phil notices his mother has put a freshly baked raisin pie on the sill to cool. Little raisins have dropped off. Looking around and seeing no one, Phil happily pops small black raisins into his mouth, sweet and with thick sugar.

Abruptly, he cries in anguish, "Uggggh!"

In his mouth is the vilest taste he has ever known! He plucks it out to examine it. What he thought was a raisin and bit down upon turns out to be a moth. He NEVER forgets this terrible taste.

Keep growing up, Phil, but watch out for danger.

~~~~~~~

The enormous generating station on the river at Pointe du Boise has high steel doors on the side. Railroad tracks lead down the steep incline so the engines and cars can go right inside. One Sunday, his older brothers convince Phil to ride the little speeder car down the embankment.

"It will be great fun, Phil, just like flying."

Quickly they pop him up on top and put their shoulders against the speeder and shove him off down the rails.

"Go, Phil, go!" they shout.

He hurtles toward those towering closed steel doors.

Little Phil becomes terrified as the speeder goes faster and faster and faster.

The older brothers suddenly realize what they've started and become scared, too.

They shout, "Jump, Phil, jump!"

"I can't," wails little Phil.

More and more speed, more and more terror. The doors are getting closer and closer. The speeder connects with a heart-stopping crash, and Phil is thrown off into the gravel.

At a town meeting the next day, it is divulged that the culprits are the three brothers. The next meeting is with two angry parents and three small sons.

~~~~~~~

Poles over their shoulders, one sultry summer day, the Three Musketeers walk to the river to fish. They skirt the herd of cows in a field on the way. Jim, the eldest, is in the lead. He is the dreamy one, presently lost in his thoughts. Chuck and Phil are behind, whispering.

Jim is peacefully progressing when he hears, "Mooooo, mooooo." Phil and Chuck thunder their feet, pounding them on the hard-packed field. Jim drops his pole and tears across the field for the fence, preparing to jump over.

When he realizes it is only his brothers, he shouts, "Jesus, you scared me. What do you think you're doing? You could have given me a heart attack."

~~~~~~~

Phil says he brought his parents to BC when he was ten years old. He is wide-eyed and in awe of the size of the ocean when he first sees it. The pungent smell of saltwater makes a big impression on this young lad.

~~~~~~~

Phil did grow up into the happiest, sunniest soul ever. He made it through all his childhood adventures, and he was my favourite adventure, too. He considered life to be a great gift. He made it only to age 68, but he put every ounce of living and laughter into those years. And I try every second of my own life to emulate him in this.

We always said when we couldn't fly anymore, we would each get a Harley Davidson and, when we couldn't ride them anymore, we would each get a motorized scooter and race them.

Yes, he started out as a child, but had he been given the chance, Phil would have been a wonderful, happy, and hilarious big OLD kid.

CHAPTER THREE

Selecting the Right Day

Sometimes a small thing can change an entire life ~ like selecting a different venue, or sometimes even selecting a different day.

The first time I watch Phil with his vintage airplane, it is like watching the god of airplanes. At least the god of airplane walk-arounds, and I feel a bit of godly worship. Oily rag in hand, heavy aviator leather jacket, with only the long white silk scarf and goggles missing, he touches and strokes every part of his airplane as if he might be with a lover.

Because I know it too, I know he wants nothing more than to be already flying, but he conducts his airworthiness check carefully, methodically, and with intense focus. Tenderly, he runs his fingers over the leading edge of the propeller, checking for nicks that could crack a prop that turns faster than the speed of sound.

From my ground school classroom window, I see Phil's World War II Harvard every day. I make the smudges on that window. Although I love all aircraft, above all, I love the Harvard. It is tied down ~ just outside there ~ so close. I would give anything to go for a flight in this beautiful airplane, but I am afraid to approach the pilot, even though he is my husband's friend. I have known Phil since I was 13, but still, I am scared to ask.

I often see Phil taking passengers, and every day I want to ask if he might take me, but I am too shy. I would offer to pay for fuel in exchange for a flight. Perhaps today I can be courageous enough to walk out to speak with him. But no, again, not today. Maybe tomorrow?

Each time he returns from flying, I watch him make his traditional low, fast pass before circling to land. And every time, I can almost taste a flight. My heart flutters and pounds. He is the accomplished pilot, and I am, quite literally, a fledgling, just trying out my wings.

I go on flying my school's small Cessna and continue to dream of the big Harvard. I may not EVER get up enough courage to ask.

~~~~~~~

But then one cold, bitter day, I do manage to summon my courage and, shyly, I walk slowly, dragging my feet, across the frozen grass to the taxiway and then, at last, ask.

Picking this day was not auspicious.

I approach Phil as he works around his airplane. Then I notice his hands are blue from the cold.

This huge airplane has circles of red, white and blue on the side of the fuselage, looking like a bull's eye. The extended glass canopy glistens from his polishing. There is a vast expanse of yellow wing. It was built in 1940 and used as a wartime trainer.

Then, very hesitantly, I say, "I would love to go for a flight if perhaps you might take me some time."

He moves easily for someone so big. He steps toward me.

Instantly, and with twinkling eyes, he smiles underneath his long mustache and says, "I am going now. Come with me."

I can't believe my good fortune. He shows me how to climb in. First, I must stand on the wide wing then turn backward onto the foot-hold attached the round belly of the aircraft. The stretch feels longer than my legs. I swing up, then over the side, directly onto the leather seat before slipping deep down into the rear cockpit.

I am enchanted. I take a deep breath of leather, oil, and grease. I find I have a complete set of flight instruments and a control stick between my knees.

I listen carefully when Phil says, "This is how to release the three-point harness. Should the airplane ever roll-over, this is how to escape."

Roll-over? I think, but I don't say, "Well, let's hope there will be no need of that!"

Then Phil stands on the wing and cranks the inertia starter handle, like drawing a heavy bucket of water up out of the well. No simple turn of a key for this aircraft! While the starter continues to revolve, he leaps in quickly.

From the open front cockpit, he shouts, "Clear prop."

It's a warning to anyone nearby that the propeller is about to turn.

When the 600-horsepower engine fires up, I see flames burst from the exhaust just over the wing. Yes, flames. Clouds of smoke are fanned backward around this massive yellow aircraft. There is a terrific roar, followed by many backfires.

Phil says, "My favourite sound ~ is yellow."

~~~~~~~

In my headset, I listen to Phil.

"C-FMTA taxiing to runway 29."

He holds the brakes firmly, and he applies maximum power to the massive engine. The power increases, and at the very last moment, Phil releases the brakes so that we roll quickly and lift off with such force it takes my breath away. I feel the bump as the wheels retract underneath us up into the fuselage. We are away.

We gain altitude and fly up the coastline, ocean frothing from the wind and sparkling like diamonds on our starboard side, mountain ranges towering on the port side.

Phil says, "How do you feel about aerobatics?"

"Fantastic!" I say.

Phil explains everything he does and says, "First, I will climb to three mistakes high, then we'll begin."

He starts with spectacular rolls. Next comes thrilling and sensational loops. I become totally disoriented, and my eyes and brain struggle to locate the horizon. Where is up? Which way is down? This is the biggest thrill I have ever known.

We skim stunning glaciers like icing on a cake, speckled not with sprinkles, but with skiers. We wave our wings from side to side, and they wave their brightly coloured mittened hands back at us. We are so close. I can see them smiling.

I am shocked when Phil says, "Would you like to fly?"

I hesitate, but the temptation is too great, and I cry, "Yes, yes, I would, please, I would."

When I take the stick, I discover that this large aircraft responds amazingly delicately to controls, and I love every minute before Phil says, "I have control," and takes over again.

It is a tremendous first flight in a Harvard, and I am sad when we have to return to the airport. Phil's landing is perfect. It is not an easy aircraft to land. There is a saying that if you can fly a Harvard, you can fly anything. He absolutely kisses this huge airplane onto the runway.

Yes, a perfect landing, but only for a second. When he applies the brakes, they are locked up. We have been flying in the wicked cold at high altitude, and the brakes have become frozen.

Phil shouts to me, "Lee, hang on!"

Instantly, the aircraft leaves the runway and careens with tremendous speed across the frozen field. There is a terrible crash as the airplane falls into a deep drainage ditch just before the tree line. The tail comes straight up behind us from the force. In a fraction of a second, we are vertical, the entire airplane balancing on its propeller. In the second it takes when the airplane must decide to continue all the way over or come back, I taste great fear. My view on either side of Phil's head has so far been blue skies, but immediately it changes to green grass as we point straight into the ground.

We balance there for a few brief seconds then crash backward, breaking off the wheels.

The plane sits on its belly.

Quickly Phil is releasing my harness and is pulling me up and out of the cockpit.

He says, "Stand back, back here, in case there is fire."

I stare at his airplane, such a picture of beauty, strength, and perfection a second ago, but now everything is mangled and twisted.

I can't believe we have survived. There is too much shock even to cry. I want this day to disappear. My heart is broken. Though I shake all over and my knees will hardly carry me, I go to Phil, reaching up to hug him, to comfort him. It is agony to see his distress at this catastrophe. This aircraft is his entire world, and now it is very broken.

Soon I hear sirens and think, "Oh no, someone else is in trouble," not realizing the sirens are for us. Firetrucks, ambulance, and the police arrive.

Paramedics take our vital signs. Accident reports are filled out. I am in shock, and the RCMP drive me home.

Later Phil phones my home to speak to his friend. He says, "Are you sure Lee is okay?"

The next day the pictures of the wreckage in the newspaper make me feel sick. My colleagues at work tiptoe around me in sympathy.

For two weeks, my body can hardly move from being slammed against the harness at such velocity. Bruises are everywhere.

~~~~~~~

It is a long time before I hear from Phil again ~ maybe a year, but my heart sings when one day I hear the throb of his airplane overhead my farm and experience wondrous joy in its return from its rebuild. I am immensely relieved that Phil flies again.

I race my truck to the airport, seeming unable to get there fast enough. I stand with my fingers entwined in the wire, clutching the security fence, hoping to see Phil and his airplane. It turns dark, and I continue to wait. I wait but, though his headlights brush my face, he races away with his mechanic co-pilot, who has flown with him to bring the airplane home again. He does not even see me there.

Life continues for each of us.

Our future is unknown then. It's a mystery.

We know not yet that a lifetime of ethereal, all-encompassing, and great happiness together awaits us. It seems this event has somehow linked us already. We have no way of knowing our relationship will one day deepen beyond belief, and this first flight in the Harvard is only the first of many, many, many flights together ~ flights of the aircraft ~ and the flight of our two hearts.

~~~~~~~

And because of this intense happiness, I now know I selected the best day, after all.

CHAPTER FOUR

An Elegy of Words

When you enter into the vows of marriage, do you anticipate this is this beginning of sharing? Sharing, not just things and dinner, but sharing thoughts. Sharing words. Not always words of importance, just everyday things, ordinary things, but sharing nevertheless.

In this new relationship, I am immediately and consistently devastated. We never talk.

I suffer loneliness relentlessly. Loneliness is a dark place, like being in a dark room every day, where someone has slammed the door and left with the key.

And if there is no sharing of words, even after years of tears and begging for conversation, you no longer wish to be there. It is a lonely place when the response is always the same, always: "I don't know what to say."

~~~~~~~

I find myself too long in this place and, at last, I give up. I never knew this person anyway. How could I?

Something in my life has to change, or nothing in my life will change.

I want to say, "You closed yourself off from me," but I don't. I just leave. I close the door and leave without the key.

I don't then know precisely what I want. I only know I want to talk to someone. I want a lot to talk to someone and for a long time ~ for a lifetime. Yes, please, for a lifetime.

I believe life is meant for sharing. The best way to share it is with words. Words that are easy and flowing from the heart without design or prepared thought.

My favourite quote is:

A Definition of Friendship

Friendship is the comfort
The inexpressible comfort
Of feeling safe with a person
Having neither to weigh thoughts
Nor measure words
But pouring all right out
Just as they are
Chaff and grain together
Certain that a faithful, friendly hand
Will take and sift them
Keep what is worth keeping
And with a breath of comfort
Blow the rest away

When I am alone again, I doubt I will find what I am seeking. Perhaps I am destined to be alone, but being alone by choice is different from being alone with someone. Being alone by choice means there is no longer the hollowness, the emptiness.

And then ~

One day I find a world of never-ending words with Phil.

Phil and I talk easily. Phil and I talk effortlessly and endlessly. We talk about flying, it's true, but we talk about both trivial and important things, too. We talk about important things that matter to us. There must be a lot of what matters to us because we never stop talking. We learn about each other this way.

Phil says, "I want you to get to know me."

And then when I do know Phil better, I explain, "Phil, I need to tell you my stuff."

Phil listens carefully. He doesn't immediately give his opinion. He takes time to give careful consideration before delighting me with his thoughtful response. He tells me exactly what he thinks, how it is he see it, never telling me what he thinks I might like to hear. Great trust is instilled in me, more trust than I have ever had in anyone in my life.

My relationship with Phil is the deepest of love stories. I honour his life, I honour our life, and I honour the life he gives me.

Phil is tender and sweet for 18 years, even when suffering from a terrible disease and being in great pain. He talks to me continually while creating jigsaw puzzles, one after the other, on the dining room table, to keep his mind off the pain. He doesn't just talk. He jokes ~ one joke after the other to take his mind off the pain.

Phil talks about his life philosophy. He believes that everyone should be who they want to be ~ who they want to be and free to do what they want to do. He is the most non-judgmental person I have ever known.

Phil's love letters are filled with exact words of our closeness and joy and are written with great beauty.

People recognize our closeness. Even when not talking at all, we communicate.

After dancing the night away one evening, while the band is packing up, a stranger who has watched us dancing, approaches our table.

She says, "I am in my fourth year of university. I'm taking non-verbal communication. I want you to know that you two have it."

Our conversations last deep into the night. I don't want to sleep. I love Phil talking to me. We talk for entire days on every subject imaginable.

Every August, we snuggle in blankets on the grass in our backyard, waiting for darkness so we can watch the meteor showers. Imagine the non-ending conversation while we wait. I am enchanted. Imagine falling asleep there.

When we have been together for many years, we decide to get married.

At our wedding, there are six people ~ a perfect number. We are in our own delirious little world of happiness this day, anyway. During our ceremony, Phil speaks to me exquisite words he has written. I cry. He cries. Words, precious words I will never, ever forget.

One day we camp on a remote island. Phil finds a small blue triangular piece of wood. He sticks a candle to it, to create lighting in our tent for our nightly Scrabble game in the wilderness. Again, words. Words are our game. This tiny scrap of wood accompanies us on every airplane camping trip from that moment on, even on our five-month trip across Canada. The words of Scrabble are just relevant.

When I clean out Phil's lunch bucket two years after his death, I find all the notes I have put there plus a tiny bundle of sticks I tied up in a shiny gold ribbon. I can't remember the significance of the sticks, but I am reduced to tears that Phil kept both them and my words.

Staying too long at the Texada Island beach one night, we have no light to see the long, long trail back up to our tent.

Phil gives me words of instruction.

"Put your forehead against my back. Walk in step behind me. I will pass a long stick back and forth in front, so we don't walk into the stinging nettle patches."

I adore his intensely protective words.

Words are Phil's greatest strength. He shares his sense of humour not only with me but with everyone we know. Ours is a life of constant hilarity.

How I became so fortunate to know Phil, I will never know, but I remain eternally grateful.

I believe it is unnecessary to separate myself from Phil and his words. Every day now, I continue to love him and remember the gift of his love ~ and his beautiful words.

CHAPTER FIVE

Can I Ever Be Happy?

What if you are deeply unhappy and what if someone comes into your life and your life is changed forever? Has this happened to you?

I yearn to be happy. I have been unhappy for too long and then~

~~~~~~~

"How are you doing with your studies, Lee?"

Phil enters the classroom where I bend over my thick flying textbook, my flying bible. I don't hear him enter, and I quickly look up to see this giant of a man who occupies the entire room.

He has come to my ground school, pretending to be interested in my studies. He puts his big hands on the edge of my desk and leans in. He is interested in this, but I find out much later he is interested in me. At that time, I am oblivious, completely unaware. I am flattered, though, that he has come.

Phil is enchanting, so sure of himself, and so happy. He is big, but also gentle. He wears the worn leather jacket of a long-time pilot, worn from countless flights over many years. It's casually unzipped, and the collar is turned up.

Will I ever be as happy as this man is?

He interrogates me and, after many questions, he is out the door again, closing it softly so I may return to my struggles to instill all this knowledge into my bursting head. He is off for a flight with a passenger waiting at the plane. It will be an exciting adventure for this passenger, and I am envious. Phil has an airplane that all pilots love.

I have been unhappy for a very long time ~ for too long ~ and yearn for happiness. Something in my life must change. If nothing changes, nothing changes. Can I summon the strength to change my life?

It would appear I can, for I soon find myself living alone. It feels like the first time I have been able to think, really think. I contemplate my new life now as I watch the moon and the stars and maple leaves in the skylight above my tiny bed.

Then one day, as I am leaving the local market, Phil is suddenly at my truck window.

"How are your flying lessons going?"

"Well, it's hard, but I am learning a lot, and I have done my solo already."

I have never talked to ANYONE for FOUR HOURS before, but we have so much to say to one another that four hours pass in a flash. My neck begins to hurt from twisting sideways to talk for so long. It is all flying-related, and I think I learn as much from Phil as I have from my instructor.

Although I don't remember it, Phil says sometime around then I invited him to come for coffee, but he said to himself, "Sure she wants me to come for coffee, but she didn't even tell me where she lives."

I am completely absorbed in learning to fly and can think of little else. I race my truck for my lesson every day the weather is flyable. I make progress with my cross-country flight. And, with my flight examination passed, I spend every second of my non-working life to soak up and assimilate every detail required to pass my dreaded exams.

Once I accomplish this, I see the world more clearly and can, at last, relax.

Time passes and, though I am happier on my own, happiness still has not settled into my psyche.

~~~~~~~

We are standing at the airport one day, just talking, when Phil surprises me with, "Would you come for breakfast with me?"

Wow!

Knowing how much we always have to say to one another, I say, "Yes," and look forward to the day immensely.

One early morning, we step down a flight of stairs into a secluded little coffee shop. We are the only ones there. It is a delightful breakfast, full of aviation talk, but our eggs and hash browns are mostly abandoned. We are engrossed in this conversation and, it seems, in one another.

As I listen to him, I think about Phil being such a happy soul. I hope to be that happy, one day, that happy.

"Let's walk," Phil says.

We pick a provincial park and walk for hours that day. Phil teaches me a marching cadence song from Air Cadets:
> *I left my wife in New Orleans*
> *With 16 kids and a can of beans*
> *Sound off 1, 2*
> *Sound off 3, 4*
> *Sound off, 1, 2, 3-4*

We march through the forest, singing our song like crazy people, ignoring inquiring glances from fellow hikers, who make little detours around us. We laugh and laugh and have a wonderfully fun time.

I feel so happy. In fact, I have never felt this happy.

~~~~~~~

Is it possible to fall in love so quickly? I did THAT DAY.

~~~~~~~

Although we know we are in love, we live separately for the next two years. Phil has a rented duplex auto-court style house. It's ancient, but it is on the beach. We have many family gatherings on that beach. We take family photos on the piles of sandy logs.

I rent a 193 square foot converted single garage, but I love it there. My wooden-shingled miniature house has a sewer transfer station on the corner, so, appropriately, it has an adorable sign by the front door that announces my little house as "Pooh Corner."

My house is so tiny that we call the little bed a trundle bed and everything except the bathroom is in one room. There is a small bar-sized fridge and a mini-oven. There is no towel rack, so one day we carry an unwieldy tree between us down the road.

People in their yards ask, "What are you doing with the tree?"

We wedge it floor to ceiling in the bathroom so I can hang towels upon its branches. Shiny glass French doors make my room very bright. Sunlight dapples the red tile floor.

One summer night, we haul the single mattress out to the attached greenhouse and sleep there. The next morning my landlord, who is much younger than we are, surprises us by appearing at the greenhouse door.

"May I come in?" he asks.

He sits on the floor with us, perfectly comfortable, and pays us a social call. What unexpected fun this is.

Phil's waterfront house is small, too, but much larger than mine. Almost every night and in all seasons, we light a fire on the beach to cook dinner there. On summer nights, we curl up in our sleeping bag to sleep behind logs on the sand, smiling when people walk by and don't even notice we are there.

I am intensely happy now, and my memory is vivid around one precious day, one of the happiest days of my life, when Phil says, "Come with me."

He takes my hand, and he leads me away by ourselves to a field at the end of the runway. He has rolled up his shirt sleeves, and his very hairy chest is visible behind the three undone buttons. I have no idea what he wants.

We pick a bouquet of buttercups. Phil takes them from me, and he makes a ring of them to put in my hair.

With soft dewy eyes, he says, "I want you to marry me."

Right there, in the tall grass, we have our own intimate "wedding ceremony." To ourselves, we are now married.

"Will you move in with me, Lee?"

"Yes, yes, yes!" I cry.

Our beginning is a fairytale, but then so are all the years we have together. It is a life full of fun and romance with much talking and endless laughter. We do everything together. Our time is exciting and exquisite.

I get my wish, and I change entirely ~ from unhappy to intensely happy, and I consider myself blessed to be with Phil for 18 beautiful years.

CHAPTER SIX

Our First School Together

When Phil and I are still very new to each other, I take him to my daughter's house so they can meet one another.

On her street is the junior high school Phil and I attended at the same time many years ago. When we leave my daughter's house, Phil pulls into our long-ago schoolyard.

"Why are we stopping, Phil?"

"Come with me," he says.

No more explanation than that.

We walk down the side of the gymnasium, memories flooding back.

Around the next corner of the school at the shop wing, Phil points to a chain swinging between steel posts.

He says, "Right there is where I first saw you."

"Why didn't you say hello?" I ask.

Phil says, "I was too shy, and you were with a bunch of girlfriends."

In amazement, I wonder how he remembers that moment from so very long ago.

I am utterly enchanted.

CHAPTER SEVEN

Under the Wing

Do you have a fear of wolves? Of snarling wolves with long fangs and molars designed for crushing. What if the wolf is very close and there is nowhere to run?

~~~~~~~

One hot summer day, we are packing for our first airplane camping trip to Tofino airport.

"Phil, I know there are lots of bears in Tofino," I say, "But are wolves there, too?"

I am a little concerned. I have seen wolf paw prints before.

"We can ask the weatherman when we get there," he says, passing off my question lightly.

I look at all the camping gear on the grass, spread around Phil's big yellow Harvard. Piles of this, heaps of that. We wedge the folding bicycles in first. It's a small opening in the fuselage, and the bikes just barely fit, but we need them because the airport is so remote. We're not able to carry the weight of much food, and we will need to pedal the twenty kilometres from the airport to Tofino for more food.

As I hand Phil bags, little totes, now the sleeping bag, so he can stuff them all in, I'm thinking about wolves.

After filing our flight plan, we take off, climb out and are, at last, heading for the west coast. It is a majestic flight twisting through craggy and rugged mountains, still encrusted with frozen lakes even though it's late August.

Forty minutes later, we touch down. This airport has three five-thousand-foot runways, but we select the most secluded spot we can find just off a taxiway. There are wide swaths of short pokey alpine heather on either side with clumps of bush and a thick forest of fir and alder trees behind. Phil swings the airplane into the heather to a lovely spot in this beautiful wilderness. There are no other campers, just us.

We have a front-row seat for watching inbound aircraft. On the far side of the bush, there is a man-made water-landing ditch for planes on floats.

We unpack and set up the tent under the wing ~ a small beige army pup tent barely large enough for two. Heather clumps make finding a suitable spot difficult, but we heave a few boulders to create a little barren area. As Phil pounds the tent pegs in, the sound echoes back from the thick forest.

I'm alert for wolves. I keep a wary eye on that line of trees behind us.

Before firing up the one burner camp stove to make dinner, we take a walk to speak with the weatherman about wolves. The weather station is a large white-painted building with many paned windows. It's a cheerful place now in summer, but I think it is perhaps not in the lonely winter when wild winds blow here. A fenced-in area contains an array of sophisticated weather-sensing equipment.

The weatherman does not give an encouraging report at all when he answers our question.

"Wolves? Yes, wolves are a problem. They have been taking even dogs recently, one from someone's porch."

We walk back to our camp quietly discussing what precautions we can take. Besides keeping our food safely inside the plane, we are uncertain about wolf deterrents.

That night, before we cuddle into our fluffy sleeping bag in our very thin nylon tent that offers little protection, Phil walks a circle completely around the tent and the plane, carefully marking our territory with urine. Will this keep the wolves away? We can only hope.

In the morning we hike far into the bush to dig a deep, deep pit for a latrine. After each use, it is refilled with sand and covered over with branches and leaves. We are surprised to find as much sand at this twenty-four-metre elevation as there is on Long Beach itself. We leave no trace. Phil is very particular about this. Every day, a new pit. Every day, a different location.

It is a short walk to the gravel road that leads us to Long Beach. We walk the beach for hours and days on the smooth, sparsely-populated sand, watching the surfers attempting to stand up on their boards in the billowing mist of the rollers.

I watch for wolf prints in the sand. I watch for wolf prints and wolf shadows melding with the gnarled salal bushes. These bushes never get a chance to stand upright but are blown over backward like the curling waves themselves from the strong coastal winds. Excellent places for a wolf to hide, I think.

In a few days, we have exhausted our meagre food supply, so we pull out our funny little bicycles with the tiny wheels for the ride to town for groceries and sugary things from the bakery. We shop for aroma-free foods without strong wolf-enticing smells.

~~~~~~~

This life is easy and relaxing, and one early morning, Phil is lazing in our sleeping bag. I'm up before him. In these cramped quarters, I sit now with my chin upon my bent-up knees, my back to the zip-up screen. We are just inches away from one another softly chatting, planning what we will do this day.

Suddenly, Phil's eyes dart past my shoulder to "something outside." Simultaneously, he raises one finger to his lips, signalling silence. He points to whatever it is ~ that "something outside."

Slowly, so slowly, I twist with tiny, precise movements.

All my concern regarding a wolf sighting is justified now. It becomes a reality before my eyes.

How I manage to stay motionless, I will never know. I forget to breathe. I am stunned. A huge wolf is loping out of the mist in the trees directly toward us into the morning light. Quickly, he is entirely in our camp.

Airplane wings must be tied to the ground, and the wolf is very interested in the tie-down rope on the opposite wing. We watch under the belly of the airplane. He circles the rope, sniffing and sniffing our scent.

His fur is thick and white, gray and silver. It is shiny like it's oiled, thicker on his neck. Each paw is enormous, like a serving platter. He radiates intelligence. His amber eyes are narrowed. His short ears are pricked forward with interest.

We keep still. We keep silent. How has he not seen us just inside a tent screen, so incredibly visible and close? I tremble and wonder if he will, at any moment now, see us.

But when he has satisfied some mysterious curiosity about our scent, he slowly continues in the same direction from whence he came into our camp and into our lives.

Now we move, rolling quickly onto our bellies with noses pressed against the screen to watch, disbelieving and thoroughly enchanted, as he trots without haste and without effort, fluidly, across the wide taxiway. On the other side, he stops at the first bush he comes to, lifts his leg on it then, like good poetry, he melts into the bush.

We stare at one another wide-eyed. We're speechless at first. Jaws drop. How could such a thing have happened?

I quickly scramble back into that sleeping bag with Phil, laying my head on his shoulder, wanting to feel his strong arms around me now. We whisper about our chance encounter with His Royal Highness, this beautiful stately wolf.

He is where he belongs, in nature, free and wild, and he has given us the gift of his beauty.

Very up close and personal. We think few people have been so close to a wild wolf.

For eighteen years, we camp at Tofino Airport, but we never see another wolf.

My concerns are over. I never have wolf-anxiety again after this incredible encounter on an extraordinary misty, magical morning under the wing.

CHAPTER EIGHT

Texada Tradition

Today the tide has come in, and there's something special to us that's lost forever. We have a ritual we share passionately, but now, we can't.

~~~~~~~

It's Friday night, and we're just home from work. Quickly we pack our flight gear: headsets, kneeboards, map, and a cushion to boost me up high enough to see through my cockpit window.

Into the truck goes the tent and sleeping bag. We are going airplane camping on Texada Island, a beautiful place to go where people are few and wilderness is plentiful. We choose this location frequently, as it is only a twenty-minute flight from our home airport, accessible at the end of a long workday before night falls. Landing must happen before dark here since there are no lights at this remote runway.

I lift off, and our world changes dramatically. Such freedom it is to fly. And two entire days are coming up just to enjoy nature and each other!

We eagerly anticipate our traditional Saturday night dinner because it includes a ritual important to us.

Pilots fly on the "eight hours from bottle to throttle" mantra, so, of course, there is no sip of wine before leaving home Friday night and no wine before flying home Sunday evening.

However, there is wine for Saturday night, and it is special to us. We drink our wine out of the same cup, and it is magical. It is not a wine glass. It's not one glass for each of us. In fact, it is not a glass at all. It's a simple green plastic coffee mug, its white logo half worn off long ago, but it is ours, and it holds significant meaning. It means love and contentment with one another. We take turns drinking from the same cup.

We offer the cup to one another.

"Here, your turn," holding it out toward the other.

It is symbolic of our shared life together.

We have decided to take the "little" airplane this evening. She is a beautiful little bird, all bright and shiny green. Snowy white, like the feathers of an owl, she is an elegant flyer. She will hold four people, but we have removed the back seats so we can take camping gear.

I usually prefer to fly her, but sometimes bend to the dewy-eyed look in Phil's eyes when he yearns to fly her, too.

It is a stunning view from three thousand feet above an azure sea, treed islands all around, little harbours filled with sailboats and pleasure craft bobbing there, having settled in for the night. The sailors are camping, too, but in their yachts.

The scarlet sun is lowering behind the hills now. Hurry little flyer, get us there before darkness sets in.

We touch down gently, watching for deer on the runway, and roll into the field. Wings are tied to a long anchored steel cable so that if a wind comes up during the night when we sleep, the airplane will not be blown over. Quickly the tiny beige pup tent is set up under the wing and our sleeping bag installed while we still have light.

Tomorrow will be a familiar routine we have done a thousand times, all leading to the sharing of that mug of wine together.

We sleep deeply that night in the fresh air. No traffic noise, no sirens. Just us and privacy, alone in the field, no one else around.

After breakfast, we hoist our backpacks and head down the runway. Although we bring some food in the airplane, for anything fresh, we must hike an hour to the grocery store, off the end of the runway, through a narrow trail with tall first growth trees.

As we walk down the runway, we keep a sharp eye out in case there is an aircraft landing. Crickets love the hot runway, and they splash out in frantic black waves left and right as they hop away from us, and we nearly step on them. We don't walk in the grass at the side of the runway because later we will pick the wild strawberries there.

Dinner will be cooked over a little fire tonight, so as we tramp along the trail, we watch for old pine trees that may have toppled down. Phil has taught me how to make a fire on my own without a match, and pine pitch is a good starter. I gather tiny twiggy branches as tinder as we hike along, stuffing them into my backpack.

In the woods, we rarely see anyone else, but sometimes we see salal pickers with enormous piles of salal towering on the back of their bicycles, bulging out like loads of ducks carried on the back of mopeds in China.

Arriving at the old country store with the original wooden floors, we invariably select the same supplies for our traditional Saturday night beach dinner. Baking potatoes will be wrapped in multiple crinkly layers of tinfoil. Corn on the cob will soak in the ocean before we roast it inside the husk.

There is a butcher here, and we say, "We'll take the best steak you have, please." We also buy sugary homemade dessert treats.

For our ceremonial dinner tonight, Phil selects a little bottle of wine from the quaint miniature liquor store in a dim corner of that ancient building.

We split everything between our backpacks with all the food surrounding the only glass item ~ our precious bottle of wine.

We make the long trek back to camp then head down the three-hundred-foot embankment trail to "our" beach. Halfway down, I trip and go for a header. Though I am unhurt, we panic because the wine is in my backpack. We quickly unpack to see if the bottle has broken. Phew, it's intact.

We call this our beach because there is never anyone else there, just the sea, the sand, rocks, driftwood, and us. It is a great long crescent beach, but it is quiet today with only little lapping waves. What could be better?

Phil lets me start the fire. I have gathered together my pine pitch, my tiniest branches, my dried tinder, some slightly larger twigs, some larger again and some big pieces for later. I have my flint and steel. It is a challenge that took me some practice to master without that match, but soon, I am listening to a snap-crackling fire.

Phil takes care of the most important job of all, putting the precious bottle of wine into the sea to cool.

Then we lay back, leaning together against a big gnarly beach log, bare toes making patterns in the sand. We are shoulder to shoulder. Heads bent toward one another. Hands entwined, talking and talking, the thing we're best at doing. We watch the fire die down to embers.

We snuggle as time passes. We are enjoying shiny sea lions poking their heads up in the sparkling ocean. An osprey is diving from great heights straight into the water. We can hear his wings whistling as he rockets down before the plunge. We know the nest is up near the runway.

At last, it is time for our ritual sharing of wine from a single cup. Phil goes to the shore and wades into the waves.

~~~~~~~

Phil wades and wades. At first, I think nothing of it. But he continues to wade. Phil does a lot of wading. I begin dinner while Phil wades. Then I am curious. I see Phil's wading forming into a grid pattern. And he is getting deeper and deeper. He circles every big boulder, half as tall as he is. Dizzyingly, round and round. Back and forth, he slices through the water, head bent down, hands shading his eyes over the water to see more easily into the depths. He is searching, searching. The tide continues its relentless rise. He says nothing. I don't say anything either, but secretly I think a mask, a snorkel, and flippers would be good here.

~~~~~~~

Now he has been in the water for a very long time. The water temperature here doesn't warm much after winter. Soon he will be hypothermic. He will do anything to protect our Texada ritual. He's like that.

It wouldn't be possible to completely lose a bottle of wine, would it? But it is a small thing amongst large beach boulders.

Still, Phil says nothing, but I can see his colour rising like the tide.

I prepare a circle of stones around my small fire, flattening and spreading coals evenly around. Corn cobs roast close to the embers. Potatoes are thrown right in on top of the coals.

We have a small grate with us, just big enough for two rib-eye steaks. Has anyone ever eaten such a delectable meal? It is perfect.

Perfect, except for the wine that's lost.

It's looking like we'll have to return to hunt for it at low tide tomorrow and return to our tent tonight without our Texada ritual.

~~~~~~~

Suddenly and triumphantly, Phil plunges into shoulder-depth water and brings up that little bottle. He throws both hands into the air in a big "V" and holds his dripping, seaweedy prize aloft with a triumphant rejoicing cry of, "Here it is!"

He has an intensely silly happy grin!

~~~~~~~

You are right if you thought the wine was extra special that night. As we pass the plastic mug back and forth, his mouth to my mouth, it tastes delectable, and so does he. A delightfully beautiful romantic evening of lovingly, sharing our "lost and found wine."

CHAPTER NINE

You Can't Do That Here!

The night is coming quickly. The trailing edge of the yellow ball of the sun is dipping below the tops of the trees. The sky is a painting ~ a painting of stunning reds and oranges.

We are rushing to set up our tiny beige army pup tent under the airplane wing. There is camping gear strewn all about.

Because we're working, we don't hear the approach of a stranger until he says, "What are you DOING?"

I jump, startled by his appearance in the thick dusk.

"We're going to camp," Phil says meekly.

"You can't DO that here!" he says with exasperation.

We assume we're not permitted until he says firmly, "There are bears here!"

We have been warned.

We are at a primitive airport without lighting, so we have no choice but to remain right where we are and tell him so. He shakes his head in disbelief.

As he steps away into the night, Phil rushes with high swinging hammer strokes to pound in the remaining tent pegs. The ping-ping-ping of metal on metal echoes back from the dark woods. Quickly, we set up the tent and stow our gear.

We have planned this trip for a long time, wanting to fly my little airplane into the grass strip at the north end of Mabel Lake in the southeastern interior of B.C.

The developing resort here has properties for sale all along the beautifully manicured grass runway. Property owners taxi directly to their own front door. An idyllic set-up, we think, and we're anxious to check it out.

We have crossed the ocean from Vancouver Island, twisted through the mountains in this quest, and have, at last, arrived safely. We taxi and bump over the grass to the very edge of the runway at the end of the grass strip, near the trees.

A tiny one-burner stove provides hot soup for dinner while we contemplate the possibility of a bear visit, each of us glancing sideways at the other.

We HAVE been warned, but how will we deal with this?

Seriously, what protection do we have from bears? OMG!

We take stock.

Of significant importance is the unhappy fact that the fuselage of this airplane is not metal. It's a flimsy fabric that would make easy access for a hungry bear in search of a midnight banquet if we stow our food inside. The alternative for the food is with us in the tent. DEFINITELY NOT!!

We have been warned, but what can we use to deter a bear if it shows up? We count up possibilities.

Well, we have a small soup pot. We can clang the pot and the lid together, but we decide that would be an insignificant bear deterrent. What else?

Uhhhh, there's the hammer. We hope the bear never gets that close. Think, think ~

Oh, yeah, there's the sabre. We always carry a sabre in a rigid case. But a bear wouldn't care that it is pretty scary to look at. Again, he'd have to be mighty close.

Oh dear, oh dear, the arsenal is meagre.

We wash dishes in the pitch black by flashlight, now not glancing sideways at one another, but watching furtively every shadow in that bush beside us.

Are those eyes?

We stay up late, because of fear, I think. At last, we take a chance and crawl wearily into our sleeping bag. It has been a very long flight. After whispering our bear attack strategy, exhaustion and deep sleep eventually overtake us.

~~~~~~~

Suddenly, we both jump straight up and out of our skin at nearby dogs going insane about something. They sound like rabid, aggressive, junkyard guard dogs. I can almost see their slathering fangs. They don't stop, just going wild, a whole pack of them.

Rapidly we speed, stumble and fumble into clothes and pick up our "weapons of destruction." We sit close together, two terrified pilots in a paltry little tent, knees bent to our chests, leaning against one another shoulder to shoulder, peering out through the screen into the total blackness when guns start firing.

We are terrified beyond belief, and I think Phil wishes we had a gun right now.

Bang! Bang! Bang! And yet, more bang, bang, bang. It goes on and on and on. It sounds like a war zone. The dogs are crazed, and the shooting continues. I am sure Phil can feel my body shaking against him. We say nothing, just sit still like stones, tightly gripping our sabre and the hammer, white-knuckled, the puny little soup pot there between our knees, ready to "ting, ting." Yes. "Ting, ting" would scare a big black hungry bear, wouldn't it? Wouldn't it?

~~~~~~~

The gunshots are getting closer. Much too close, and I feel surrounded by these wildly frantic dogs. I quake uncontrollably. The sounds persist almost beyond endurance, and I am terrified that we're next.

~~~~~~~

Then gradually the volley of gunshots lessens and eventually, the guns fall silent. Men are shouting to the dogs now, calling them back. Finally, they quiet too.

Phil, my six-foot and mighty Karate Instructor Warrior, pushes the envelope of what we wish to know by slowly and silently unzipping the tent zipper to shine the flashlight around. He immediately stops that, bouncing back inside our meagre protection, as the flashlight has reflected from eyes in the bush.

"OMG!" I whimper with a whisper.

He says, "It is probably a deer."

"Yes, yes, probably a deer," but I notice a barely perceptible tremble in his voice as he's doing his best to sound confident.

After hours of vigilance, we tire again and cautiously, we crawl back into the sleeping bag, this time fully clothed. We lie on our backs, eyes wide open, each clutching, white-knuckled, an ineffective weapon to our chest.

My ears are more alert than they have ever been before, listening for paws padding closer and closer and closer. It is so quiet that I can hear my pounding heartbeat.

~~~~~~~

When I wake up, I am surprised to be still clutching that hammer. It is a warm and beautiful dawn. Weapons can be laid aside at last.

The man who had kindly come to warn us last night has returned this morning, checking to see if we've survived. With our thanks, we hand him a freshly brewed cup of camp coffee. He warms his hands around the cup and says, as we knew, that the marauding bear was there, but they hadn't managed to shoot him. Did they try extra hard, knowing we were in a little tent extremely closeby? Maybe.

~~~~~~~

A close call puts a higher mark on the gratefulness scale, and this morning, we can relax to enjoy the extreme beauty of this area. It is bliss to sip morning coffee with a lovely feeling of intense thankfulness that the bear made his rounds only of the sturdy wooden residences and NOT of the airstrip itself. He didn't discover us with our fabric airplane, with our really thin nylon tent and our extremely wimpy weapons!!!

We didn't camp there for two nights.

CHAPTER TEN

Mr. Kanasawa

P hil is a black belt Karate instructor.
It is examination time. Mr. Kanasawa has come from Japan to conduct the proceedings.

Afterward, Phil takes the examiner on a flight to Tofino.

Mr. Kanasawa looks down on the virtually empty beach and asks, "Where are all the people?"

Phil realizes how very different things in Japan are, where there are so many people at the beach, it is difficult to find room to even sit on a towel.

CHAPTER ELEVEN

Kick It Up a Notch

Do you like to kick it up a notch and climb higher? Today is a stormy one, but we're up for a hiking challenge. We twist right, left, right, left until we crunch into the gravel parking lot from where we will begin. We back our 4x4 truck into the brush, nose outward so no one else coming to use the trail can block us in when we're away. We set out to kick it up a notch, and the hike begins. It's going to be strenuous.

I stop for a breather half-way to the top. I pull off my warm vest. It's not needed now. I tie it around my waist and wait for my breathing to calm.

Unexpectedly, as I stand to rest, I am rewarded with quite a sight. As I gaze off the trail down into the ravine, I see beyond the treetops the rooftop of a large home with a lengthy wooden deck attached. At the farthest end of that deck, there is a big wooden hot tub with half its cover folded back. It looks like it's waiting. Then, just before I turn, I catch a blur. Unbelievably, there he is ~ a man streaking naked across that long wooden deck. Quickly, he places his hand on the edge and vaults horizontally into the steam, right up to his neck.

I blink. Did I really just see this?

Oh, yes, it's going to be a good day. Already it's been kicked up a notch.

On the trail up, we are surrounded by the Garry Oak trees for which this park is famous. We hike on the north side, and our path winds happily around green groves of moss-covered boulders that never see the sunshine.

When we reach the top, we thread our way close to the drop-off. We sit on the very edge, legs hanging down. We are at only two hundred and forty-five meters above sea level, but the boats still look tiny far below in the whitecaps.

There are stunning views of Nanoose Bay, which is a six-kilometre deep-water bay with a pretty estuary at the head. Looking south, we see Lantzville, even parts of Nanaimo.

There is the military base directly below us and moored in the bay, there used to be a decommissioned yellow submarine floating for many years.

We have a picnic of a French loaf with different kinds of cheese and fruit, a red checkered cloth on which to place our small feast.

There is a phenomenon I have never seen before. I know that fog and clouds can form instantly when the temperature and dew point are the same, but I have not witnessed it before.

As we sit high on this rocky promontory, clouds are forming right before us, at eye level. They last for a minute or two, moving with the wind to the west then dissipate like magic, all within the same few hundred yards, renewing this magical scene over and over again.

That alone would have been enough of a show to kick it up a notch. But now there is a little miracle we had not anticipated. Suddenly we hear a familiar sound ~ the heavy whop, whop, whopping of an enormous Sea King Helicopter ~ approaching from the west. This definitely kicks things up yet another notch.

As this huge military aircraft lazily comes into view, we see that the side doors are open, and men are sitting on the deck with their legs dangling out in the air, just like us. Like the clouds, they are at our eye level too, and they grin while they wave. They are so close that I swear I can see a little tear on a knee of a flight suit.

Slowly, slowly, they hover then settle down to the circular landing pad at the military base below. We are speechless at our good fortune to be here this day and at this opportune time.

So, we've achieved our hike this day to the top of the rock and, oh, and can you guess the name of our mountain? It's quite fitting. It's called The Notch.

CHAPTER TWELVE

A Tale of Two Braces

Have you ever had trouble getting approval for a mortgage?

Now I know that free advice is worth every penny you pay for it, but let me offer you my two cents worth at no charge.

~~~~~~~

But my free advice is to recommend you avoid mortgage stress! At least the kind I had.

Phil and I live in a rental auto court right on the beach. It is a happy place, as happy as we are to be together if you disregard the mushrooms that grow in the shower. It is a hut more than a house, but we love it. A bouncing baby mortgage is the furthest thing from our minds.

We have mismatched days off work, so I am often on the long stretch of sandy white beach with the children. I talk to them and admire their sandcastles. One day I show them a tiny expired octopus I found in the tide and scooped into a jar.

We have an outbuilding laundry and a miniature garden. We feed the multitudes of birds. This happy house is a furnished place with a bouncy bed that springs around when an earthquake happens.

~~~~~~~

"Rental is a waste of money," says my ex, who is still a good friend. He advises Phil and me, "Buy a house, for Pete's sake."

We hunt for houses so hard we are ready to give up. None are as appealing as where we are now living. Mostly, we wonder why we would leave living on the beach, even though it does make financial sense to buy a house.

Then, on the occasion of looking at just one last house, before we take a break from house hunting for a while, we walk in the front door of one last house.

We take one look at each other in the entryway mirror, and Phil grins as he calls to our realtor, "How do we make an offer?!".

We haven't even looked through the house, but we know in our hearts that this is the one!

The house smells of heavenly homemade bread, which we later learn is a trick used to sell a house fast, and these owners are so anxious to sell. They accept our offer right away. The listing has only been on the market for two days.

But here's the crunch: We had to state "subject to financing," and I must procure this financing on my own. Panic sets in. Will I qualify?

However, I go to see my bank manager and enjoy the woman taking the manager's place while he is away. Quickly the mortgage is mine, proving it to be an "easier than I thought it would be" endeavour. We are over the moon.

But, just as quickly, I receive a call from the manager himself saying they made a mistake. I do NOT qualify for a mortgage.

OH NO! This is the house of our dreams. We hunted so hard to find one we loved, and now it will not be ours after all.

To say we are shattered is to trivialize the state of our minds. What do we do now?

This is the perfect house. It is clean; it has a large yard: it's small and is a single-level without stairs – a home we can age in.

We are fortunate to have a realtor that has noticed the large shed on the property is too close to the property line, and the Board of Variance causes a slow down in proceedings.

You wouldn't think we would be at all happy about this interruption, but it is a gold bar of treasure. It grants me extra time to scheme some means of a mortgage.

While the Board of Variance dithers, we plan, make phone calls, and think hard, but nothing is working. We come up empty. We are going to lose this house.

A few days later, after we have exhausted all our plans of action and have worn ourselves out, I return home from work, a routine day, but today my head hangs low. It hurts to know we have been unable to procure a mortgage.

I turn off the highway onto our country lane, tail between my legs, and filled with sorrow. It's hard to get our hearts set on something unattainable.

I rattle my old truck along in dejection.

I pass the farm that I pass every day, the one with the long rutted driveway, and today I'm surprised to see that, at the end of that dusty road, seated at a card table, is a very small boy. I think he is too young to be out there alone. He is perhaps six years old. He sits behind his small table, selling bags of something.

My mind is heavy and elsewhere, and I continue ahead.

~~~~~~~

But wait a minute. I need to stop. I feel an overwhelming need to go back. Suddenly I know it is important to return to this small boy.

I pull over into the tall, roadside grass and walk back. He is a towheaded youngster, so timid and sweet.

"Hello," I say. "What do you have here?"

"Plums," he says.

We'll probably never be able to eat them all, but ~

"I would like two bags of these lovely plums, please," I say.

When he stands up to put the money in the tin, I nearly burst out in tears. There, beneath his shorts, are two thin little legs that are completely encased in long shiny metal braces, even about his tiny knees.

We smile at one another, and I thank him.

A minute later, when I walk in the door of our beach hut, I find a voicemail message from that very same bank manager saying he has reconsidered, and the mortgage will go through after all.

~~~~~~~

I look every day after work for my small friend, but I never see him again.

Perhaps ~ perhaps, he has sold all the plums.

CHAPTER THIRTEEN

Jumping Curb

We wander lazily and slightly wobbly on a hot summer morning. You on your second-hand bike. Mine's second hand, too. The deli and liquor stores are on the left and the hardware store on the right. Our quiet town of Qualicum Beach welcomes us and other Saturday errand-runners, everyone looking happy to have a day of leisure.

Suddenly you look back over your shoulder and shout, "Lee, hey Lee, watch this!"

Everyone hears and looks, including me. You look left then right before racing across two vacant lanes as fast as an older bike rider can go, with boyish intent to jump the curb.

You do not jump it. Your front wheel strikes the curb with vicious force, your back wheel pivoting straight up in the air, forcing you perilously downward, almost perpendicular.

Miraculously, you smash back down before going head over heels.

I am delighted you have not been hurt. So is the little crowd you have attracted. Only when I see you are okay, does this scene become funny.

CHAPTER FOURTEEN

Two Rings

Can you guess how long it takes to carve two rings? Will there be time?

Phil has walked slowly and purposefully toward me. He stops. Something about the way he looks at me makes me look up at him in wonder. Gently, he lowers himself to one knee ~ and proposes! We have lived a long time together, so I am not prepared for this! He says he wants us to get married as soon as possible! Little did we know.

Oh my gosh, how do we plan a second marriage? What do we do? We're not good at this.

He wants to visit my Dad. I haven't suspected why. My Dad tells me later that when I leave the room, Phil says that he would like permission to marry his daughter. Do old-fashioned men of this integrity still exist? It certainly appears that they do.

There is a very special person, our close friend, who we want to marry us and when we contact her, she has only one date that is available before she moves on to a new calling.

It is very soon. Can we pull this together in time? It absolutely must be her, so we strive to get everything quickly in place.

It is crucial for us to have Native hand-carved wedding bands. We want eagles for strength with hummingbirds for love. We choose a carver and visit her studio. We tell her of the extremely short time-frame, but she says she can do it.

Please, hurry!

At a family picnic, we steal my daughter and son-in-law away behind a hedge to tell them our news and ask them to stand up for us. My daughter is so ecstatic that she jumps up and completely spins around before alighting again. We ask if their daughter, our tiny granddaughter, can be our flower girl.

This is a totally secret wedding we tell them! It will be a wedding in our back yard with just them and my Dad.

Even though we are worried about the completion of our rings, we work hard to organize everything else.

Phil and I shop together for a dress for me. He sits on a tall stool, analyzing every dress I try on. Yes? No? We laugh. His favourite is the one that is marked down and marked down again from summer, and is only nineteen dollars. He loves this white one with eyelet!

I sew bohemian crowns of flowers with tulle and tiny roses for we three girls.

We are becoming very anxious about our rings now because we have heard nothing! Is it too soon to start worrying? Have we given our carver enough time? How can we get married without our precious rings?! I call and leave a message.

Too soon our wedding day is only a few days away, and still, we have heard nothing. I place another phone call and, yet again, get no answer. I leave another message. We hear nothing.

Eventually, our day almost here. We think we will be cunning and drive to the studio, but there is no response to our worried knocking. We peer in the windows, but all is black as midnight. This is when I know we will not get our rings.

We are stricken. Returning home, I am in tears. How can we get married without our rings? All this planning we've done will be for nothing.

We concentrate on writing our vows. We order a little cake and white orchids to go on top.

We keep calling our carver again and again ~ nothing.

We are both working full-time, but we continue putting everything into place, regardless of the rings, with the few hours we have left, not knowing how we will manage without the rings.

Finally, at the very last minute, our carver calls.

"Come for the rings."

We rush to her studio with great relief. They are even more beautiful than we anticipated. They are deeply and intricately carved.

As we are leaving, she puts up her hand and says, "Please wait," and disappears into the back.

She returns to lay a smooth leather drawstring pouch on the glass-topped counter. From this, she retrieves the softest tiniest downy white feathers. She tucks them tenderly all around our wedding bands in their box.

She explains these are special feathers. The Tsimshian chief has blessed them himself. She gives these treasured feathers to very few, she says, just those that are special to her. We are intensely moved by this gift.

Now we are standing face-to-face and soul-to-soul. We are married under our backyard arbour in an emotional ceremony. Though we are smiling, tears squeeze out and course down our cheeks as we place our treasured rings on one another's fingers. Oh, how they sparkle on this warm and sunny September afternoon.

There's a little sprinkling of humour when our Justice of the Peace asks, "Who gives this woman?" and my Dad says nothing.

My daughter elbows him and says to her grandfather, "That would be you, Wally!"

We all laugh at this and then again when our tiny toddler granddaughter takes the little basket full of white rose petals we gave her to throw and turns it upside down, snowing them all at once on the grass.

These beautiful moments make beautiful memories.

Phil has selected our wedding dance music, and we sway in the grass. The words enchant me.

"I am me. You are you. All we need is who we are."

Ours was an enchanted intimate backyard wedding.

My daughter says, "Mom, you and Phil were in your own little world that day."

It was a day full of meaning and forever-memories.

Yes, though barely in time, those two rings did come to us ~ a truly blessed gift, that wouldn't have been possible without the strong spirit of those sacred downy eagle feathers.

CHAPTER FIFTEEN

The Stone

Have you ever found something totally unexpected? Something that just wasn't supposed to be there? A treasure of monumental proportions?

Today is a sunshiny hot day. We are trekking 300 feet down to the beach from Gillies Bay Airport on Texada Island. We have done this hundreds of times before, our backpacks filled with a not-too-creative, but entirely traditional, lunch of tinned beans and tinned tomatoes, along with a can opener and one spoon to share.

At the beach this particular day, if we had decided to go left instead of right, this would never have happened. We select a lovely picnic area on this entirely deserted expanse where there is a stream headed for the sea. We jump over the stream. It seems the otters like it here, too, since it is much too smelly, so we pick up our gear and head farther down the beach.

In a pristine spot now, Phil puts our backpacks behind a massive round rock, taller than we are, a perfect place to keep our water cool.

At home, Phil has a collection of arrowheads that makes me jealous. I have always wanted to find an artifact of my own.

I notice Phil has become busy with something.

Teasingly, he says to me, "Hey Lee, I will find you an artifact."

He has spotted a large stone with marks. It is triangular and extremely heavy, and I watch as he pries it labouriously from its face-down place in the beach gravel and props it into a standing position.

We stand open-mouthed and stunned as we see a large face carved into it. It is incredible, and our eyes bulge and blink in disbelief. It is huge. It's two feet high. There are high cheekbones, protruding eyes, a flat nose and a mouth like the Easter Island head carvings with a chiselled oval around the face and what looks like a headdress at the top.

This find is heart-stoppingly exciting. We spend the rest of the afternoon planning how to retrieve it! We estimate its weight as somewhere around 200 lbs. Much too heavy for the airplane. We place it back where we found it, face down, and scatter branches and small logs over the top to hide it.

We fly home and continue to plan how to rescue the stone. We decide to take our truck, canopy, canoe and camping gear and camp on Texada Island.

At 5 a.m., we launch the canoe and paddle an estimated seven miles back up the island to the stone. This stone is awkward, and it is almost impossible to manoeuvre such a dead weight. We lift it over the side of the canoe, and somehow, pink with exertion, we manage to lift the monster over the gunwale without puncturing a hole in the bottom of the canoe.

On the return paddle, the wind comes up, and we become concerned for our safety and that of our precious cargo. However, we make it back to our campsite, then tug and drag our treasure on a tarp up the beach gravel to the truck for its journey home.

We are astounded that only because we selected this particular spot, and Phil was making a joke, this mysterious stone artifact sits now in our living room, a most prized possession.

It's not aboriginal. They carved in wood. Could it be Viking? Will we ever know?

CHAPTER SIXTEEN

Passion for Flight

When you board your airplane and stand tippy-toe to stuff your carry-on into the overhead, do you wonder about the pilot seated just upfront in the cockpit? The pilot who will fly you through the skies? Do you think about the number of years of experience? What the pilot's background is?

Phil begins his yearning with cardboard "wings" tied to brown little five-year-old boy arms.

He calls to his brothers, "Come and watch me fly. I can really fly."

As they crowd around, he leaps off six-foot rocks in this Manitoba childhood. He wants flight, and he attempts flight, but every time he tries, he lands at the bottom in a crumple. He is five years old.

He yearns to fly. He wants more than anything to fly, and as he grows older, he tells his father, "Dad, all I want is to learn how to fly."

When he reaches the right age, he joins Air Cadets. He is with his two older brothers. Air Cadets quickly becomes his whole life.

It is a life filled with intense training in flying skills and marksmanship. He matures and learns decision-making, leadership.

Phil has such a passion for flying, and he works hard enough that he earns the only scholarship available. It is for a summer of flight training in Chilliwack. He is only seventeen.

Flight training is an exciting life. The cadets live, work, study, and breathe flying all day, every day with ground school classes in the morning and what they're here for, flying every afternoon. They share barracks and eat together in the mess hall. It's a serious business, similar to being in the Air Force.

Every student that makes his first solo flight receives the debatable pleasure of a bucket of water over the head from his mates.

Phil has wanted to fly since he can remember, and his greatest happiness comes when he earns his Private Pilot License that summer.

Returning to school in September, he is the only licensed pilot in the high school.

When he returns home, his Dad drives Phil to and from the airport. Phil is a fully licensed pilot, but he can't drive a car. At the airport, though, Phil is in charge. He rents the plane. He is the PIC, the pilot in command, and he flies his Dad around for an hour.

Inevitably, renting an airplane is not a long-term solution to Phil's dream. School finishes and Phil is now working full time. He spends his days off looking for a "light" aircraft to purchase. However, he is unable to afford a plane by himself, so he takes on a partner. "Light" airplane doesn't enter into the equation when Phil hears about a massive yellow WWII Harvard Warbird for sale. This 600-horsepower trainer is far from a light aircraft. He and his partner swing the deal.

On the day the airplane is delivered, Phil is working the night shift, so he has the day free. He stands anxiously, shifting from one foot to the other, waiting, waiting for the plane to arrive. His partner is not there.

The delivery pilot pulls the canopy cover over the cockpit, smiles, and hands the keys to Phil.

Phil is now alone with the plane ~ alone with the plane and unable to fly it.

Phil looks at the keys in his hand. They seem to burn there. They feel wonderful. The plane is theirs ~ all theirs.

It is a hot summer day. Heatwaves shimmer from the asphalt. Phil walks around and around the plane. He pulls the canopy cover off again, just to savour her beauty. He slides the many-paned and glistening canopy back. He runs his hands over every flight surface. He checks the tires and the propeller.

Slowly, he climbs up onto the wing and then quickly into the front cockpit. Everything is beautiful ~ the instrument panel complex, the smell of leather and grease surrounding him in a happy cocoon. In a dream, he slowly inserts the key into the ignition. He sits there in the cockpit for hours, oblivious to the raging sun. He memorizes all the instruments and the flight controls. He studies the thick manual page by tedious page.

Yes, he is a pilot, but he has not received training, nor has he been checked out on this aircraft, a requirement of the Department of Transport. That will happen next week when the check pilot can meet with him.

He thinks, *"Now, I can sit in the plane, or I can sit in it and listen to it. What harm could there be in just firing up?"*

He contemplates this possibility for a long time.

Finally, it is too much for him, and he yells, "Clear prop."

He turns that key. Billows of smoke pour from the huge exhaust that runs over the starboard wing. After coughs and sputters and backfires, it settles down. The engine runs at a terrific roar at first, but then it runs smoothly.

Phil sits here, engine running, and thinks to himself, *"Since it is running, perhaps I could just taxi up and down the taxiway."*

He advances the throttle and enters the taxiway. This goes well. The controls handle easily.

This plane is called a "tail dragger." The tail must be lifted to take off.

Phil talks to himself. *"Well, it wouldn't hurt just to try lifting the tail wheel, would it?"*

He taxis back and forth up and down the taxiway, lifting the tail to horizontal, and then putting it back down on the ground. Lift, drop. He figures it out.

"Well, this is going extremely well," he thinks.

The temptation is overwhelming.

Suddenly, he makes his decision, speaks to the tower, and enters the runway.

In a surge of power and excitement, he takes off!

All the mechanics and other pilots come streaming out of their hangars at the sound of the Harvard climbing out. It is a rare and beautiful sight.

Phil begins shaking like a leaf. He makes one circuit around the airfield, exhilarated.

But now for the hard part. He tries to land. However, he is forced to do a "go around" because his speed, angle, and flaps must be coordinated to land at all. He has never flown such a large airplane. No one has shown him how. He begins to shake violently but begins to talk to himself.

"Okay, okay, you know what you are doing wrong."

He makes circuit after circuit, attempting to land. Uh-oh, the fuel gauge! His fuel is running low. He must land – and quickly. The gauge registers lower, then even lower as he repeatedly tries to land. He sees that there is not much fuel left now. How long will it last?

He makes yet another circuit and, at last, with everything synchronized, he successfully brings the precious aircraft back down to the runway.

All the air mechanics and pilots who know him are watching this magnificent feat. Once he is safely down, they en masse throw their hats high into the air and cheer.

He did it, yes, but after he shuts down and steps to the ground, he finds his rubbery legs barely able to hold him up.

~~~~~~~

I know you are up there still, flying the skies, my love.

Every eagle I see is a reminder of a great pilot with a great passion for flight.

CHAPTER SEVENTEEN

Dreaded Meeting

Slowly I stir, becoming softly and gently aware that it is morning time. Not yet. I don't want to open my eyes just yet. With eyes still closed, I stay still and listen to sweet songbirds outside our open bedroom window. Before I even look, I picture the sun-drenched gossamer curtains that are too long, sweeping the floor before billowing out toward our bed.

Increasingly, I gain awareness and know I am with my beloved. He is big, and he is warm. Then my reverie is shattered when I jolt awake with the memory of the meeting I have at work tomorrow, a Monday afternoon meeting. As a manager, I must make a presentation and, though I have prepared, I am dreading it. Oh, today will be so long. How will I ever get through this day?

"Good morning, sleepyhead," Phil whispers.

His big calloused hand is on my cheek. He knows about my awful dread of tomorrow's meeting.

With gentle kisses and nibbling of my lower lip, he murmurs, "How would you like to run away for the day?"

Phil is so sensitive about all things concerning me. Only Phil, in my entire life, understands every nuance of my being.

"With you?" I say. "Anywhere."

I can forget my concerns. This is my day of freedom from worry.

Preparing for a flight, we check the weather and file a flight plan. We take off for a day in Powell River, a small coastal town on the mainland.

It is a lovely day of bright blue and puffy white clouds. Crossing the water from the island is a stellar experience. We watch the beautiful thickly-treed islands with little ribbon roads, the sandy shores, and secret coves with boats lying at anchor. We notice the barges pulled by tug boats loaded with enormous multi-coloured shipping containers from all over the world. We see immense cruise ships that churn up white v-shaped wakes behind them heading to and from Alaska.

We touch down gently, tie down the plane, and swing our light backpacks over our shoulders, etching the gate code in our minds so we will be able to return through the gate that is kept locked at all times.

We head for lunch at Hooters, but not the kind of Hooters you're thinking of. It is just named for owls. Dessert here is delightful. It's called Worms and Dirt, chocolate mousse with a gummy worm squirming up out of it! Yum.

For a while, we wander slowly, window shopping in the quaint oceanside town. It's Sunday, so everything is all shut down. It doesn't take long before we're hiking our favourite forested trail. We know this long and beautiful trail well. It is squishy in the marshy areas and dark under the canopy of trees. The birds and squirrels seem a little quieter than usual today, and after a time, we realize why. As we trek along, it is growing darker and darker. Suddenly we realize that this much darkness is not from the trees. Rather, the weather is closing in.

"Oh my gosh, Phil, we need to head for home. Now! I can't miss the meeting tomorrow afternoon!"

We hurry back to the airport, but, in the time it takes us to walk back, the storm is arriving with full force.

Phil says, "We will go out just long enough to have a look at the weather to see if it is flyable."

We quickly take off. Almost immediately, the storm pushes us down.

I am in the rear cockpit and looking at the back of Phil's head six feet in front of me. I am immediately terrified because all I can see is white. White ahead, white above, white starboard, white port. If I were to open my canopy, I could almost touch its thickness. I can see, almost feel, the frothing ocean below, whipped into cresting peaks from the wind. The airplane tosses and my headset is bashing from side to side and hitting the glass canopy.

"Turn back, Phil, turn back," I cry when simultaneously, he already is.

Then this monster storm pushes us down even more. I have all dual flight controls in the back, with the stick between my legs, and I am shocked to see flight instruments indicating our altitude continuing to drop since we must stay below the clouds. My heart is in my mouth.

Typically, we would be climbing to three thousand feet, but we have been forced down to three hundred feet above that dark, threatening ocean turbulence. The only way is down because climbing into clouds without visibility is the most dangerous thing a pilot can do. Mountains live in the clouds.

We are sweating it out. There is every chance that the clouds have swirled down and around the airport, and we will not be able to return to the runway. My eyes are searching, searching for a break.

Amazingly, luck is with us. As we reach the shoreline, the overcast lifts, and just in time, the runway becomes visible.

I have known pilots to kiss the ground after a scary flight, and the idea fleets across my mind.

This was a freak storm. When we called for the aviation weather in the morning, there was no mention of it at all.

~~~~~~~

And what now? Here we are, stranded. There will be no flying out of here this day.

The meeting! I am an integral part of the meeting tomorrow, but I doubt I will be able to make it in time. I am glad we are safe, but I feel sick about tomorrow.

We pull our yellow-duck raingear out of the baggage compartment and struggle as we attempt to don it in the whipping wind. This is before the days of cell phones, and we trudge off to find a telephone.

Eventually, we secure accommodation for the night at a B&B, but it is a long distance away, so we walk back to the airport again to retrieve our "transportation" ~ our little folding bikes. We head out, all decked out in baggy yellow raingear flapping furiously around us while we pedal on small bicycles with tiny wheels, flap flap, like trained circus bears with rain-streaked faces.

Will the storm pass so we can fly out early tomorrow morning? I must be at this mandatory meeting by the afternoon. I can't let myself even think about what the bosses would do if I don't make it.

After being welcomed at The Beacon B&B, we hang our sodden gear in their garage to dry out before eagerly settling into our lovely room.

We sleep heavily after such a harrowing experience.

Just imagine waking up in a strange place to the heavenly smell of homemade bread. Our hosts have been up hours before us. Reluctantly, we drag ourselves out from the soft comfort of the puffy eiderdown.

We enjoy a breakfast like no other we have ever had before. There are jars and jars of homemade fruit and berry jam, each with a spoon, every enticing kind. There's fresh fruit, and muffins, eggs made any way we would like, even Eggs Benny, if we choose. There are bacon and sausages. It looks so heavenly, and I wonder how the legs can even hold up such a heavily laden table.

We pedal back to the airport. The skies are clear again, and we can wing our way home.

I can make that meeting after all, but my husband sure has a unique way of taking my mind off things.

CHAPTER EIGHTEEN

Eagle

Phil is flying his Harvard up-island and comes upon an eagle just gliding along. He avoids the eagle but is relatively close. When the bird sees the big yellow airplane at his side, he panics and back-paddles frantically.

That same evening with company over for dinner, Phil is mimicking the motion of the bird's wings, swinging his outstretched arms in reverse motion vigorously while seated at the dinner table. The velocity of his demonstration sends his chair and him right over backward onto the floor.

The next time we have dinner with the same friends at their home, all the dining room chairs are standing except the one lying on the floor with a sign on it that says, "Phil, this one's for you."

CHAPTER NINETEEN

To Live is to Lose

Have you ever lost something meaningful? Something so sentimental, there's nothing that can replace it? It's vanished. Gone. You might have no part of it left, or you might have half of it, making the memory harder ~ a tangible reminder of the loss sitting there in your palm.

~~~~~~~

"Oh my god, Phil, it's gone," I say, sobbing my heart out.

Phil wraps me in his big, warm arms, trying to console me, but I am distraught. We have landed back home after a week away airplane camping in our little pup tent at Tofino airport. I make the long climb down from the cockpit. I pull off my headset and feel that one of my earrings is missing.

I shouldn't have worn those earrings on this trip. I should have chosen a less precious pair. I have not lost any old ordinary earring.

It is one of a pair of silver eagle feathers, a gift received when I got my license because "I fly like an eagle," and Phil knows how much they mean to me.

Nothing calms me because I know there are a million, maybe a zillion, places it could be. We have hiked, biked, and walked for hours on the Long Beach sand. We've camped in the deep wilderness heather for the week.

Time goes slowly by, Phil tells me we will look for this tiny silver feather, but I know it is hopeless, and I am heartbroken.

Oh, why did I wear these earrings this trip?

We have taken Phil's airplane this time, an old aircraft that has cockpits with strips for our feet, but underneath the strips, it is entirely open to the bottom of the fuselage. Can this microscopic silver feather be down there?

I am crushed, knowing that taking the airplane apart to search through a maze of flight controls and wires just to look for such a small silver bit is more than out of the question. It would be ridiculous.

We check through the crevasses in the leather seat in the rear cockpit. No.

We look all around in the grass where the airplane is tied down. No.

Back home, we check through our bedroll. No.

We check the totes of equipment. No.

We shake out the tent. No.

It is truly gone. Would replacing it, even if we were able to, mean the same as the real one? Would I still fly like an eagle?

If only I hadn't worn these earrings this trip.

Phil is confident and says we will look when we are in Tofino next, but my heart knows I will never see it again.

I cannot believe how slowly time passes without any sign of this tiny, precious gift.

Days extend to weeks. Winter comes. Weeks become months, all of it unflyable because of bad weather. Spring arrives before we can file a flight plan to Tofino again.

Phil, only Phil, in the whole wide world, has not forgotten the tiny earring and says we will search everywhere we had been last time. This was months ago, and I think this is a high hope he has, and remain convinced that I will have only the one forevermore.

I have not forgotten either, but in my heart, I know it is hopeless for there are miles of runway, acres of bush where we hiked, and many miles of beach at Tofino where we had been. Plus, we rode our circus-bear-tiny-wheeled bicycles for long journeys into town. We hiked on a gravel road where we would never see such a small thing, though once I did find a quarter on that very dusty road.

We take the bigger airplane again, and I am dejected already because the area we are to search is just too immense, like searching the moon. Sadness fills my heart.

If only I hadn't worn these earrings that trip.

Phil is so determined we have written down all the places where we will retrace our steps from our last trip. The list is long, and I am not feeling at all hopeful about this questionable adventure. I don't say anything, but know that in the months that have passed, everything must be covered with decayed autumn leaves.

Phil lands, then taxies, leaving the pavement to bump the airplane through the rough heather, stabbing one brake hard to swing the aircraft around.

He assists me out of the rear cockpit, down onto the little foothold, down onto the wing before I jump to the ground.

As he holds my arm, he says cheerfully, "Don't forget we want to look for the earring this trip."

I look around, bewildered. The wild heather creates an immense field of sea green as far as I can see. As I gaze despondently at this vast wilderness, I think, "impossible."

Suddenly, he reaches straight down between his boots and shouts, "Here it is! Right here!"

If we had been a fraction of an inch north, south, east or west, he would never even have seen it.

And now, I am certain that I can "fly like an eagle."

CHAPTER TWENTY

A Fine Friendship Flowers

Phil walks into the room with a very hairy chest. He walks out with a very hairy chest and a tattoo.

Tattoos are for decoration, I think, but Phil's tattoo marks the spot where they will direct the radiation.

As the radiologist begins, Phil asks, "Do you smell something burning?"

Everyone in this room, where the doors are two feet thick, freezes with panic. But Phil, as always, is joking. With great relief, doctors and technicians resume breathing.

Our oncologist is beautiful and the same age as we are, but she looks thirty. She is sensitive and extremely caring, and she has become our friend since we see her so often now. She has ordered radiation for Phil's liver tumour, which is the size of a large apple. It has spread so far it has wrapped around his lung lining and his heart, too. Radiation is an attempt to halt this monster, mesothelioma.

We believe in our friend, our oncologist. We believe the radiation will work.

Chemotherapy continues relentlessly, first one cocktail, then another, then yet another. Our oncologist is trying everything she can. Some treatments cost $8,000 per infusion.

Every treatment day, our oncologist checks in with Phil. Then, since we are word people, we spend treatment times, often eight hours long, doing book after book of crossword puzzles. So he doesn't have to move his arm, I face Phil in his big chair, printing our words upside down while the poison, like ocean waves, continues it's endless waves of drip, drip, drip.

We believe in our friend, our oncologist. We believe the chemo will work.

We have become close to her, so I make her an elaborate card of thanks for all her excellent care of Phil. She has it framed then hangs it in the big treatment room.

It is typical of our friend that she alone is responsible for the massive containers of flowers that grow on either side of the entrance to the Cancer Clinic. She plants them herself to bring a little joy to the patients, with a rainbow of colours for each season.

There is always time during our meetings with her for personal discussions. We learn she has fallen in love, and we are joyfully happy for her.

We believe. We always believe that Phil will get well.

Phil struggles through treatment, but we keep positive.

On a routine "Oncologist Day," we are extremely distressed to learn that we will not see our friend this day, but will be seeing a different doctor. What does this mean?! We enter this strange office and sit close together, arms pressing, shaking and chilled with fear. He is already there, waiting for us.

This becomes the worst day of our lives. This new-to-us doctor is very uncomfortable and very, very sad. This is unbelievably scary. This stranger informs us with great gentleness but firmness that treatment is not working and will be discontinued.

Now we know why our friend has not seen us herself today. She couldn't. She couldn't tell us this worst possible news herself. We understand and don't blame her, but this does not make it easier, and we both sob.

We sob uncontrollably while this newcomer into our lives says over and over, "I am so sorry, so very sorry."

There is nothing to say, and we can't talk anyway. We stumble out through an entire waiting room of waiting chemotherapy patients, no longer believing. We must now become disbelievers. It is the last time we are ever there.

Only once in a lifetime, will any person ever know the experience of being sent home to die.

~~~~~~~~~~~~

I walk slowly to the mailbox one day, a sunny summer day, as hot as the day Phil died.

The mailbox key turns slowly, nothing seeming to matter anymore, but today there is a letter. Today there is a letter from Hawaii. I know only one person in Hawaii. Our friend, our oncologist, has taken a new position there.

Her beautiful handwritten letter begins, "My dearest Lee, I am writing to see how you are since your unthinkable loss of Phil."

Friendship can flower in the most unusual of circumstances, and those friendships are a sweet gift to be treasured in the heart forever.

CHAPTER TWENTY-ONE

Pat's Love

Phil's cancer moves to the outside of his body as well. It makes a deep open sore in the center of his chest that requires dressing changes every second day.

As the end draws nearer, the nurses come to our home, but before he is too sick to go to the Health Clinic, we travel there for these dressing changes.

His usual nurse is Pat. Sometimes Rhani.

Phil makes them laugh throughout the process of changing the dressing. One joke after the other. He must be the brightest spot in their day.

If one can be joyful on such a mission, Phil makes it that way.

One day at the clinic, Phil is in his usual position, sitting sideways on the high treatment table, legs hanging down.

It is a routine day, routine procedure until Nurse Pat stands between his knees, looks him directly in the eyes, puts both her hands on his shoulders, and says, "Phil, you have added such quality to my life."

It is an intimate moment, one that I am honoured to share. I am sure she loves him, and I am not surprised.

One day Pat calls to see if she can come to visit. She arrives with gifts. There is a sweet photo of herself and Rhani taken at their staff Christmas party.

The second gift is in a wooden frame, a beautiful quote:

> *Some people come*
> *into our lives and*
> *quickly go. Some stay*
> *for a while and leave*
> *footprints in our*
> *hearts and we are*
> *never ever the same*

Pat becomes our close friend throughout these many long months of treatment.

How could I ever be jealous that she loves Phil when I completely understand.

Phil, you left footprints in Pat's heart.

CHAPTER TWENTY-TWO

The Lives Phil Touched

Has anyone ever changed you? Profoundly and forever changed you? I lived an unhappy life, and then I met a man who touched the lives of others, and when I tell you, you, too, may never forget him.

Do you know, Phil, that you have touched the lives of others? You would not think that about yourself, but you have.

Your parents constantly laugh when we are all together because you delight them so. All your brothers do too. Our families and our friends.

My daughter will not call you stepfather, but she loves you so deeply it is easy to tell by her enjoyment of you and her enthusiastic hugs. Our granddaughter loves her Poppa, always resting her head on your shoulder, and phoning to see if you will play Speedy and Slowly Gonzales accents with her.

One of your nurses leaves a gift at the front door one day. She has asked you, as you are dying, if there is anything you wish you had done in your lifetime.

You reply that yes, you wish you had taken me to Paris for lunch.

She leaves all things relating to France with an incredibly tender letter, saying, "Since you can't go to Paris, I will bring Paris to you."

We both nearly sob to find there are wine glasses, an Edith Piaf CD, an Eiffel Tower poster.

Chemotherapy clinic is a serious place, but every nurse adores you because you make them laugh.

Your doctor's sympathy card, sent to our home, says you were an inspiration to him. All his words are beautiful, and he calls you amazing. That your doctor has written means the world to me.

But no life has been more influenced than mine.

I changed dramatically from the moment we were together. Going from extremely shy to more outgoing, you gave me confidence for the first time.

I stopped worrying because you told me I worried more than anyone you have ever known.

I learned to laugh and take myself less seriously.

I began to sleep, having the marvellous experience of joyful exhaustion.

You taught me everything you knew. I learned many things only guys did, and you were incredibly proud of me when I achieved them.

You had me re-roof our house with you, paint it throughout, lay new floors, and build raised vegetable beds by myself. I felt, and still feel, competent.

When we were first together, my life changed from one of relationship-silence, causing deep unhappiness, to a bright life of laughter and constant conversation.

We whisper. We roar. We act silly and, sometimes, we're serious.

You taught me about romance, the beauty of tenderness, the enchantment of submission.

You gave me a legacy of life, Phil, and I will love you forever.

You whispered into my ear and my heart. You kissed my lips, and you touched my very soul.

CHAPTER TWENTY-THREE

Private Museum

It is very comforting to know Phil's Harvard now resides in a private museum in Ontario.

It has been completely restored, right down to the bare metal and rebuilt. It has new glass, new instruments, and a pristine fresh coat of yellow paint.

They tell me it is better than new. Phil had always longed to do this.

The Harvard lives in a hangar. You can eat off the floor there. Phil always said, "You can't fly a hangar."

I hope he knows his Harvard has now been restored.

Part II

LEE

CHAPTER TWENTY-FOUR

Running Away

Have you ever wanted just to run away? Me, too. I want to run away whenever the going gets rough.

I move to a farm with my family when I am only six years old.

~~~~~~~

Running away first occurs to me when I am six-years-old. I hate school. My poor mother bundles me up on school days. Anxiously, because she knows what is coming. Then she quickly tucks my baby sister into her buggy before I can run away and hide somewhere.

We live near the city, and she has to walk me to school. Every day she picks a new switch ~ a branch that is long and thin. It feels like a whip, and in my mother's case, she uses it to make me go to school. I hate school.

Crack, crack, crack against my poor little self to make me go to school. I dawdle, holding back. I try to run away back home ~ anything to avoid that school. Thwack and thwack again. This was the beginning of my wanting to run away.

My father, being a war vet, is given a steal of a deal on an old house on thirty acres of nothing but scrub and trees ~ everything changes. At my next six-year-old school, I love school.

We have a coal-heated house, and I dress rapidly in front of the oven set on high, with its door open. It's the only way to keep warm in the chill. I swallow breakfast quickly so I can run down "Lee Lane," a trail cleared through the trees by my grandfather.

I run like the wind, joyfully, arms akimbo, lunch pail and hair flying through the thick, dark woods of forest then down, down, down the steep hill to the big yellow school bus that carries me to my precious new school. This is like running away every day.

There is a wooden stile halfway down the trail that my grandfather built, so I am not ripped apart by the multiple strands of barbed wire fence spaced closely together. I run up four steps, across the top, then down four more on the opposite side. I am alone. Yes, at six. I run and run and run. At home, my mother listens from a half-mile away for the sound of the horn, the big friendly bus driver blares to tell her I am safely aboard. Beep, beep, beeeep! I think now that she must have heaved a sigh of relief ~ first, because I made it safely to the bus, and second because I am gone for the day.

~~~~~~~

On our farm, there are eight cherry trees. Cherries we enjoyed, sweet juice staining our peach fuzz childhood chins all summer long. In her own version of running away, my little sister lived in those trees ~ halter-topped and pedal-pushered. She was not actually a monkey, only looked like one with skinny little arms hanging from branches. She just hated to be called out of her trees for dinner.

Our big red barn is a magical playground! First, there was just the old Farmall tractor in there, but eventually came the horses. We didn't own the horses because we couldn't afford horses. They were "loaners."

We ride all over the countryside, young and very often alone. My every ride is like running away, which satisfies some inner urge.

Our mother nearly has a heart attack every time my sister's horse would come home without her. Her horse knows how to knock her off. He ducks under low branches. Once she's off, he turns around and heads back to the barn where he knows he gets fed.

Shhhhh! Every Christmas, I get up early ~ before anyone else stirs. I boil the kettle and lug it out to the barn. I make numerous buckets of "Lee's Special Christmas Breakfast" for each horse, fit for kings. Or, maybe unicorns.

Oats and bran, beet pulp, carrots, and flax seed. On top of it all, I drizzle thick treacly molasses in "S" patterns then stir everything labouriously around with a huge wooden paddle, heating everything through with the hot water. They like this so much I wish they could speak, but it doesn't matter, a nicker says it all.

When I am twelve, I receive my first bicycle for Christmas. From then on, I spend a lot of time running away. Freedom!

I am given a little broody hen with a clutch of eggs. She hatches all twelve into the tiniest fluffiest little walnut-shaped yellow chicks. She is a doting mother, always with wings spread like a tent over her tiny babies. However, the percentage of roosters is high, and soon the barn is full of a large flock of full-grown roosters!!! White guano is dripping from everything.

Dad says, "Get rid of those roosters!"

I would have liked to run away, hating to dispatch any, but I do my duty.

I plant my first garden. The deer think I have planted a salad for them. The deer dine on their salad. My heart breaks and I feel the need to run away again, but I don't. Instead, I decide to sleep next to my garden. Perhaps a human scent will keep the hungry deer away.

My Dad won't let his little girl sleep alone in the wilderness with her garden, so he cheerfully sleeps in his sleeping bag next to me. Am I the only youngster to have a Dad like this?

~~~~~~~

When we are small, one day, mad at our mother, I really am determined to run away. I pack my little red suitcase, flinging in blue jeans and shirts in a fury. Then I pack my sister's much smaller little red suitcase. This is it. We are going! I take her by the hand, and we're away. I take her everywhere with me and now to run away. Out the door and down the back steps we go.

Half way to the barn I suddenly stop. I set down those little red suitcases, right there in the dirt.

I go to the orchard and pick apples. Then I pick poisonous mushrooms that grow all around. I light a little fire in the yard that goes snap, crackle.

I find a battered old aluminum pot. I chop everything up, put it in my pot and stir with a stick. I cook a heavenly fragrant stew, but this is a deadly concoction, and I keep my sister away!

~~~~~~~

I don't know why running away was always so important to me. I haven't figured that out yet.

~~~~~~~

These are my memories of life some time after covered wagons and a long time before a man walked on the moon.

There were a lot of things done in those days that we wouldn't do now, all of it considered too dangerous. But we survived, perhaps thrived.

It's a life I still treasure and wish every child could know.

A life that was not worth running away from. Or, maybe I didn't actually want to run away.

Maybe I just ran away because we had little red suitcases.

That's what you do with suitcases, right? You fill them up, and you go away. I just never got very far.

CHAPTER TWENTY-FIVE

Cry Yourself to Sleep, Little One

There is a famous painting called *The Scream*. When I think of my little sister, I think of that painting.

Today I hear her scream ~ a scream of pain. She is only five. I sit on the wooden bench, and it is my turn next. Our father went first ~ our fearless leader.

Until now, it has been a beautiful life. Thirty acres of trees and fields to play in and a row of eight huge cherry trees of all kinds where we spend happy summers. Winters, we sled and ski down our big hill, at least when we're not down in the well with Dad, perched on the wooden platform floating on top of the water. Frequently, the pipes freeze and need to be thawed with the blowtorch. We shiver and hold the light for him.

But now, we are in the clinic to receive immunizations. We have been warned to be brave because they will hurt, and they do. Our mother has been taken away from us. She has contracted polio and is in the Nanaimo hospital. She is very, very sick.

When they transfer Mom to the sanatorium in Vancouver, my sister and I, two little waifs, stand on the hospital lawn, the wind fluttering our best dresses around us, crying and waving to our mother.

She waves back so sadly at her hospital window. She is so weak, and it takes two nurses to get her up.

Back at home, my father speaks to me privately, asking if I would like to live with my best friend, Bonnie. She lives far away in Victoria. She and I are eight years old. At first, I am excited at this prospect, since we have been friends all our lives, and I agree to go, but realize later that I likely didn't have a choice in this matter.

Dad explains that my little sister will live with our grandparents in Vancouver, and our one-year-old baby brother will live with our neighbour. All of us go away, separately, to those who will take us. Dad continues to live alone in the big old house to work and support the family. Now there is no one at home to keep the coal furnace going and the clothes mildew in the upstairs attic-like closets.

Excitement to be with my friend lasts only a few short hours. As we put my clothes into a drawer of an unfamiliar dresser and make up a strange bed in a cramped bedroom, I begin to understand what is happening.

I am young, but on the first night of my new life, it dawns me with full force that I am away from my family, and I feel, deeply, the loss of them and my familiar life I knew before. I pull the blankets up to my chin.

Terrible homesickness settles in, but there is nothing I can do. I feel like a hostage and cry myself to sleep.

I begin school ~ so many new faces. My teacher is kind, but I feel alone and scared.

After school, I am still scared. This is not my family. I cry myself to sleep.

More days without my family. Long days. Long days turn into weeks. Weeks turn into months.

There is little security with my new family. For some reason, we keep moving to different houses ~ first one house, then another, one time, an auto court. Everything is always so strange to me.

Christmas comes. Christmas goes. My birthday comes and goes. The first celebrations ever without my family.

Many months pass. Suddenly, I am told that my father will be coming to see me. Of all my childhood memories, I cannot recall one so happy as this one. I am ecstatic. I run to him and cling to him, unable to leave his side. He keeps me snuggled close. It is the first time I have felt secure for a long time. But quickly, he is gone again, my only visit in an entire year.

There are swimming lessons and trips to town on Saturdays to spend our twenty-five cent allowance for chores on towering double ice cream cones.

The absolute eternity without my family continues.

My little friend always supports me. She tells me now that there was not a night in the year I did not cry myself to sleep.

I run and play and go to school, but then the never-ending nights come, and I am overwhelmed. I am distraught for many long months. Though a new family surrounds me, I am unthinkably lonely.

I feel tremendous joy and such great relief when the news comes that our mother, though weak and very tired, can at last return home. We are to be reunited as a family, all of us coming home.

Returning home, I'm different now, having learned to live without my family. I am mature beyond my years. I have convinced myself that I am an adult and can cope with anything.

At long last, our lives return to normal. Mom never regains her strength, and we know we are lucky to have her still. My little sister and brother are at home already, and now I join the family, too. Reunited at last.

I don't remember ever crying myself to sleep again.

CHAPTER TWENTY-SIX

Hidden Deep

Something lies hidden deep within me. It's in my brain, in my heart, and it's stuck in my soul. It's a hard thing that has been there these sixty long years.

As I sit in my worn leather office chair, I feel my body flushing, now that I have decided to write it.

Can this even be written? I am too warm. I sweat. I slip off my sweater to continue. I have never talked about this ~ such a dark thing and so very painful. I force myself to breathe. Force breath in, force it out again. With great trepidation and trembling, I begin now to write.

~~~~~~~

It is a dusty, hot day. I am eleven. My little sister is seven. We have asked to be allowed to play with our friends. We live in the country, and these two friends are a distance away, so we take our bicycles. Our friends will walk to meet us halfway.

We ride toward our friends, just two little girls on red bicycles, not a care, on a rarely-travelled gravel road. We wave a greeting to our nearest neighbour, Auntie Beth, as we pedal by.

A little farther along, we round the corner to the even narrower dirt-packed laneway. Suddenly, and with shocked disbelief at what I am seeing, I freeze with fear. I swerve my bike in front of my little sister's bike to stop her.

A lion approaches us. It is incredibly close. It is not a cougar. It is a lion. It is an African lion, and it is huge. It is looking right at us as it runs toward us, its yellow belly swaying from side to side. Its enormous paws are kicking up dirt.

Our friends are hiding, trying to play a trick on us. I can hear them giggling in the bush. But the lion hears them, too. The lion stops running toward my sister and me, crosses the lane, and crouches flat to the ground. Our friend, Maureen, bursts out of the bush, intending to scare us. With one leap, the lion pounces and attacks her, bringing her down. She screams. She tries to get up from the dirt, but the lion brings her down again. She screams and screams.

I grab my little sister's hand and shout, "Run!"

We are panic-stricken.

I shout urgently, "Run faster!" as we race back to Auntie Beth's.

We scream, telling Auntie Beth that a lion has got Maureen. She seems confused but runs to the telephone.

Rapidly she phones our father saying, "Bring your rifle, Walter."

Then she calls the RCMP.

In the neighbourhood there is a zoo, a popular place with a steady stream of vehicles visiting, all of them loaded with kids. Even local children spend a lot of time there. My favourite is feeding peanuts to the elephants. It is a vast property, green-grassed, with many cages. The pungent and foreign smell of exotic animals is everywhere. There are excitable, energetic monkeys swooping hand over hand in their enclosure. There is a big kidney-shaped pool for the seals. There are lions and many birds of prey.

My sister and I wait at Auntie Beth's, trembling, hand in hand. We are utterly terrified. Dad's car careens past, fishtailing and spitting gravel.

Around the next bend in the laneway, Dad sees Maureen and the lion. He shoots, but the lion gets away.

The RCMP, the Fish and Game Club, and the entire community come to hunt the lion. Hundreds of men with rifles arrive. Cars line both sides of our remote road. There are airplanes overhead ~ searching, searching. It takes three hours before the lion is tracked down and shot.

Hours later, our father wearily takes us home. He calls my sister and me to the central pivot-point of our family, the old oak kitchen table. Dad scrapes up chairs for us and sits us down in front of him. He takes our hands in his. He is crying. He chokes, finding it extremely difficult to talk. His voice is ragged. Our lives change forever when, gently and solemnly, our father explains that the lion killed Maureen, and we will not see her ever again.

The zoo owner had not even notified the police. We are the closest families, but neither Maureen's parents nor our parents were warned of the lion's escape from its cage at the zoo the previous day. Just a phone call to surrounding families was all the owner needed to do, but no one knew. No one was given a chance to keep their children inside.

~~~~~~~

The zoo is closed. The owner is charged with manslaughter.

My sister is too young, but I must testify at the court proceedings. My father leads me into the high ceilinged stately old Court House with the highly polished marble floors and rooms that echoed. As the only witness, I take the stand, then take the oath and begin to testify ~ a terrible experience that I sob through, holding on to the polished wooden wall in front of me.

The defence lawyer is brutal. He asks the same questions over and over again ~ a difficult thing for my father to see and endure. After a lengthy trial, the owner is convicted of a lesser charge of criminal negligence.

When my little sister and I are finally up to returning to school, the bus students, our friends, classmates, and teachers treat us gently.

Years pass. Was there neither counselling available or sought? I don't know. We just suffered our loss silently.

~~~~~~~

Today there are subdivisions of lovely homes on both that laneway and the zoo property. Most people have forgotten the zoo was ever there or a child died.

I never did. Maureen's family never did. Our family never did.

Sometimes I am overwhelmed with thoughts of Maureen and need to visit her grave.

I kneel in the wet grass, sobbing, tenderly brushing bits off her headstone with my hands. I recall her screams. I speak to her, my small friend. I lay the red rose I have brought her ~ just there, beside her name.

It is small comfort that her mother was buried beside her a lifetime later. How her mother must have suffered. I was told her mother never got over Maureen's death.

~~~~~~~

My cousin says I must record this, for when I die, no one else will know its truth.

And so, it is done.

I cross my arms, holding my shoulders. I have told my story, and now I am cold. So cold. I pull my sweater back on.

I understand never getting over it.

I do not forget you, my little friend. I will not forget you ~ ever.

I'll be bringing you a rose again soon.

CHAPTER TWENTY-SEVEN

Ten Easy Pieces

It's 1959. I am 12, and my sister, Janet, is 9. We share an attic-like bedroom.

This morning as I yawn and rub my sleepy eyes and become fully awake, it dawns on me that this is Christmas morning.

Childhood December mornings are dark like velvet and hushed. Our old house is softly silent. No one is stirring, not even our new baby brother.

I lay awake a while, and then I whisper to my sister, "Are you awake?"

"Yes, but we're not allowed to get up."

"I know."

We are not supposed to get up too early on Christmas morning.

I wait a while longer then whisper again.

"Would you like just to look?"

"Yes."

We want to look because every Christmas there is one unwrapped present underneath the tree for each of us four kids.

We can't see our old worn green linoleum nor the gabled ceiling. But we don't need to see because we know this room, and we know well the steep steps with the landing halfway down, leading to the living room.

Conveniently, the steep staircase has an old carpet runner that keeps us silent. It has long brass rods holding the carpet into place. We know it well, and we know to skip the loose step because it squeaks. We sift softly down on our pyjama bottoms.

As we're doing this Christmas morning, we've done this in the pitch-black many times because recently, our family got our first television. Ever since we sneak silent down the stairs when we're supposed to be sleeping. We sit shoulder to shoulder on the bottom step behind the living room door. We take turns watching the new TV through the keyhole.

Sometimes, our dad suspects that we are there. Without warning, the downstairs door is yanked open to blind us with brilliant light, and we shoot straight up at being caught by our gleeful dad before he sends up scurrying back to our beds.

This Christmas morning, we sneak down the stairs, quiet as mice. On the bottom step, with great anticipation, we slowly open the door. We switch on the light. But we stare at the tree ~ disbelieving.

There is an unwrapped gift for each of our younger brothers. We look at each other. There is nothing for the two of us ~

nothing. We don't speak. We just tiptoe closer to the tree, nearly stepping on a raggedy frayed string.

But then I see on the floor at the end of the string, a tiny piece of paper. I pick it up. There are words written in pencil.

The note reads simply, "Follow the string."

What?

Then we notice the string continues across the living room floor, under and out the front door. We look at each other again. What could this mean? We open the door to see the string runs straight across the porch and disappears.

It's freezing outside, so we quickly run to the back hall for boots and winter coats that we toss on right over our pyjamas. Then we follow that string.

It goes across the driveway. We live on a farm. The next thing the string does is wind around a fence post, then it wraps around and around the barbed wire. More fence posts, more wire. Then it takes off across the barnyard in the direction of the big red barn.

We are totally bewildered. We have no idea what this could mean.

The string disappears under the big barn doors.

We fumble to find the light, and when it comes on, standing before us are two shiny gleaming red bicycles. One big, one small. We are awestruck!

~~~~~~~

My memory of bikes is only riding Jeannie's bike last summer. Jeannie is the daughter of family friends. She is older than I am, and she has a bike. I loved to visit Jeannie because she let me ride her bike as much as I wanted. I learned bike skills. I learned to speed around and then to stand hard on the backpedal brakes to circle and skid to a gravel-flying and dusty stop. The freedom I feel is too soon over. It's time to go home. Dad doesn't have money for bikes, and I continue to walk everywhere I go.

~~~~~~~

So, we are tremendously excited this Christmas morning as we thrust open the biggest barn door and push our treasured new bicycles out. Our house is at the bottom of a steep driveway, so together, we furiously pedal our beautiful bikes to the very top. We turn. We grin at each other.

I shout, "Go!"

We launch ourselves with as much speed as we can get ~ faster and faster and faster.

~~~~~~~

I don't want it to end, but the orchard is coming up fast. At this great speed, I know to stand hard on the back pedal brakes. But unexpectedly, I wobble terribly in great waves ~ left-right, left-right, left-right ~ because there is no resistance to my braking. My foot goes right to the bottom.

I very nearly fall right off. It is still mostly dark, and I am so busy trying to keep my balance, that I am unable to steer. At this rate of speed, I crash straight into the plum tree.

My bike ~ my first bike ~ my beautiful bike ~ explodes and disintegrates into ten easy pieces.

The front-wheel buckles in half. The handlebars twist sickeningly to the opposite side. The fender is demolished. And that beautiful stainless steel basket that used to be on the front ~ flattened.

I am cut. I am bashed and bruised, but I only think, *"How could I lose my first bike? My first and 'ever-only' bike."*

Slowly and painfully, I disengage myself from the wreckage and pick myself up off the ground. My little sister circles and comes back in shock, heartbroken and crying.

"Oh, no," she cries. "the basket is wrecked. And you wanted a basket for your newspaper route as much as you wanted a bike."

I am even more in shock and heartbroken than my little sister is, but I'm not crying because all I can think about is, *"How on earth am I going to explain this to Mom and Dad?"* I have yet to ride this beautiful machine for ten minutes, and already I have wrecked it.

I am unable even to push my bicycle. Dad has to help me carry it, one of us on either end.

What a wickedly difficult Christmas this is. I lick the wounds on my body and, more importantly, the wounds on my heart. My heart is shattered into as many pieces as my bike.

The holiday season and time itself move much too slowly now.

Eventually, though, my bicycle does return from the repair shop, and I ride it for many, many years with great joy and passion, knowing how lucky I am to have it.

I learn the hard way that Christmas morning that my brand new bike didn't even have back-pedal brakes like Jeannie's bike. Although I'd never even heard of them, my bicycle had something new. They're called handle-bar brakes.

All ten pieces of that shattered bicycle were repaired.

And this allowed my shattered heart to be mended, too.

CHAPTER TWENTY-EIGHT

Goodie Two Shoes

When you were young, were there things your parents forced you to wear that you hated? I mean, hated. I mean, you would do anything so you didn't have to wear them.

~~~~~~~

For my sister and me, it is shoes. We have an old farm and are far from wealthy.

Except for shoes. It is a strict family ritual. At the end of every August, we are dragged to town, kicking and screaming in our old worn-out shoes to get our annual two pairs of shoes each in time for the start of the new school year.

That's it ~ two pairs of shoes per year. It doesn't matter how much our feet grow. We get just these two pairs. It's probably not easy for Dad to provide two pairs of shoes each, but he is adamant about shoes.

Sister Janet and I are very young and not fashionistas yet, but we know what we like, and that doesn't include the annual dreaded, hated brown oxfords. We are forced to wear them.

One younger brother gets soft brown lace-up boots. And our baby brother? Well, he looks so adorable in his new tiny wee calf-skin white boots. I love to clean the little boys' boots. And I hate cleaning those horrid brown oxfords.

"Please, Dad, do we have to get brown oxfords?"

"Not again, Dad, please," we cry every year.

"Nobody else in our whole school wears brown oxfords, Dad, NOBODY."

Pleading doesn't work. He stands firm in his belief that his children will have good shoes.

I can still remember the names of the two shoe store salesmen. "Did" and Stan. What the heck kind of name is the name "Did" anyway? Did it stand for Didley? Maybe didley-squat? Or did it mean that "Did" did see our Dad coming? And our Dad "Did" buy two pairs of shoes each, every single year. Every August.

But "Did" did see our Dad and "Did" did sell us the two pairs of shoes each ~ every year without fail.

One pair had to be school shoes, and the second pair was "for good." The "good" shoes were beautiful, but they didn't make up for the school shoes ~ not nearly. School shoes were, without fail, dreaded. And oh, how we hated them.

Now, I know you're thinking okay, there are the hated brown oxfords, but what about the second pair? What are they like? Well, let me tell you, we love our second pair of shoes!

Unfailingly, there are always the dreaded brown oxfords for school, but always there is a beautiful second pair as well. These are either black patent or red patent leather. They almost always have a strap and a fancy brass buckle, too. We wear them with pretty white socks that turn over at the top with ruffles on the edges of the cuff.

They shine like diamonds, and we feel like princesses in them. We use Vaseline to clean them and take excellent care of them. We look forward to invitations to parties so we can wear these perfect little girl shoes. We play for hours in our shared bedroom, dressing up and wearing those very special princess shoes, turning and twirling in delight.

Winter mornings, Mom calls up the stairs, "Hurry and get up, girls. I have the oven heating."

We get dressed in front of the open oven door since there is no heat upstairs. We always leave the dreaded brown oxfords for last, but we don't have a choice.

But hatred makes even the youngest of children do awful things.

Remember the farm? We live almost an hour bus ride away from school, and Mom doesn't have a car. If we aren't on that school bus, we will be home with her for the entire day, and she sure doesn't want that with two little ones underfoot already.

Janet and I devise a plan.

"Shushhh, Janet, come here. Put your brown oxfords here in this box with mine. No, no, further down, way down, underneath the blanket."

Our upstairs attic bedroom has a deep sloped-ceiling closet. There are boxes here, useful boxes, in this dark hiding place.

"Mom? Mom?" I shout down the steep staircase. "Mom, we can't find our brown oxfords, can we wear our good shoes?"

"Look harder. They must be there and hurry up because you're going to miss your bus."

We wait for a couple of minutes to pass while we make scampering noises that sound like we are looking.

"Mom? We still can't find them."

"Damn it, then wear your good shoes, but just this once. You're going to have to run all the way to the bus today."

It works like magic, but we better not use this trick too often.

~~~~~~~

Our parents can never figure out why the tops of our shoes wear out.

We figure out that turning the detested brown oxfords over upside down and dragging the toes alternately through the gravel on our way to the bus stop wears them out faster. First one shoe then the other. Drag and scrape.

I know it's terrible, but we figure that the sooner they are wrecked, the sooner we can wear the patent leather shoes to school.

As I get older, there is a neighbour boy, Keith, who says, "Would you like a ride? Hop up on the bar."

He gives me a ride me down the half-mile hill on the bar on that bike. I drag my shoes upside down part of the way.

I feel no guilt, no remorse. The only thing I feel guilty about is ~ not feeling guilty.

~~~~~~~

Then, even older yet, my sister and I get our first bicycles. Now we drag both brown oxford toes down that hill, using them as brakes. Brown oxfords get messed up pretty good this way!

~~~~~~~

I still have a passion for shoes. I like fancy shoes, sandals, and comfortable shoes for older people.

But my favourite is my steel-toe high-top lace-up work boots. They're even brown.

The shiny steel shows right through on the toes on these clunky big boots, having worn out naturally, without any help from me.

But now ~

I love them.

Strange, isn't it?

CHAPTER TWENTY-NINE

Babies

Do all girls start babysitting at 11 years of age? Do all girls think that a new baby brother is put on this planet just for her? I did, and I do.

In my dreams, marriage, young, at 20, includes early motherhood.

First, no luck in even becoming pregnant leaves me sad and feeling hopeless, but eventually, I become pregnant. Then begins the terrible sickness. I am unable to eat anything or even keep water down. My eyes peek out of my flowered bedspread, but complete bed rest does not ease this situation. When I miscarry at four months, I am emotionally destroyed. Nothing takes away an overwhelming feeling of loss ~ not friends, not family, not anything.

I completely doubt I will ever have a child. Nobody understands. I wanted this baby, and the tears won't quit.

Years pass. I try again and have the same result with a second pregnancy. My heart is even more broken, and I am inconsolable. I hide in my house with the curtains drawn. I refuse to go out. I feel terribly unworthy.

I doubt I will ever have a full-term baby. Nobody understands. I wanted this baby, and the tears won't quit.

More years pass, and my third pregnancy is looking more hopeful, but I unexpectedly go into labour at six months and deliver my son. He lives only one day.

Leaving the hospital, I scuff down the highly polished floors of the lobby with achingly empty arms. My life is hopelessly ruined. I have a freakish fear of everything red ~ red flowers, red tail lights, red stop signs, everything red. Eventually, this passes. I know I am a failure as a mother and suffer great guilt, and the tears won't quit.

I put my baby's tiny clothes away. I cocoon myself into nothingness. He is still with me to this day. He is the only person to whom I write poems.

Now, at last, the doctors sit up and take notice. They confer. They decide I have an incompetent cervix, and with a shiny brand new procedure in 1971, my cervix is sutured closed so I cannot miscarry. My obstetrician orders complete bed rest for six months. It is agonizing, but I comply, for if I don't, he says he will put me in the hospital. I carry this baby to term, and a caesarian delivery is planned.

As scheduled, I am put to sleep before this birth, but as I extend my arm to receive the injection, my heart and soul cried out, "No, no, NO. Don't put me to sleep! I must know if my baby is okay."

Because of everything that has gone before, I am so sure there will be some problem with this child. Again, I want this baby. Please!

Hours later, I awake all alone in my room, completely terrified. There is no husband. There is no nurse. There is no information about my child.

An eternity later, a nurse answers my buzz.

With dread and urgency, I ask, "My baby?"

"Oh, you haven't seen her yet?"

"I have a baby girl?" I said.

"Oh, I think it's a girl," she says breezily.

It is an unbelievably long wait before she returns with a tiny soft pink bundle.

As she places my yearned-for child in my arms, she whispers, "She is healthy."

My little baby proves me wrong. She is so strong and so healthy that she hasn't even been in the incubator, where they told me told all caesarian babies must be kept.

I have never, never, never been so joyful in my life.

"I have waited so long for you," I tell her.

I nuzzle into my child's downy softness. I smell her; I cradle her; I cuddle her. I can't let her go. She becomes my everything in this world.

She took all my body weight to grow into perfection, as I haven't eaten in nine months, but perfect she is and gorgeous!

Life takes on new meaning for me. She is my world. I take her everywhere with me and love her ferociously.

Two years pass, and I try for another child but go into labour at five months — a tiny daughter.

My gynecologist says, "No more pregnancies. You must adopt."

I am completely shattered. My husband will have nothing to do with adoption.

I am so fortunate that this daughter of mine, now 45 years old, lives only one hour away, and I am ecstatic that I now have a precious granddaughter, too! My time with them both is never enough. I am truly blessed and, though my body betrayed me, I am, quite possibly, a very good mother, after all.

CHAPTER THIRTY

I am Determined to Have a Wholesome Lifestyle

I look at the wagon train of six trucks loaded with everything we own. Head 'em up 'n move 'em out. There is a new life waiting! A farm life and a one-hundred-year-old farmhouse, beautifully bordered on five sides by the ocean, a river, woods, a wildlife reserve, and the railroad tracks.

Just hours after our arrival on this new farm with the ancient house, the toilet quits flushing. There are many friends and a lot of family helping us this day. The bathroom has heavy usage. We dig and discover there is only a dirt bottomed septic tank and absolutely no septic field. That's big project #1 to "rectumfy" this problem.

But I am determined to make a wholesome lifestyle and forge onward.

That first night I lie in bed listening to the rats climbing up and sliding down the interior walls of this huge old house, wondering what we have gotten ourselves into.

Project #2 is rat eradication, but I am determined.

Project #3 lasts six years. We renovate. Only three screws are holding in the eight-foot windows in one room. We find walls full of charcoal from the roof having burned off long ago. The southeaster' wind from the ocean blows through the poor construction so hard that I nail heavy quilts over an inside doorway and weigh it down, so it doesn't billow up. The living room is unusable.

The old house is heated with a clunky wood furnace in the basement. We cut down trees, load rounds in the truck, haul wood to the lean-to and stack it up high. Sometimes I split firewood for whole days at a time, filling an industrial-sized wheelbarrow with a wooden tower and wobble it trip after trip from the barn to the dirt basement path, throw it all down only to stack it all up a second time.

One deep-snow winter, I am walking back from the barn and am terrified to see flames shooting out of the chimney. My child is inside! I drop two big pails of milk and race to throw my little girl out the door with instructions to run to the end of the road and direct the fire trucks while I phone. Twelve big firemen swarm the house and the attic. They condemn the furnace until it can be repaired, but there is no structural damage ~ only emotional damage.

Project #4: new fireplace bricks, but I am still determined to go on.

My young daughter begins 4H at age 9, such a small girl to be controlling a thousand-pound steer, by what seems like an insignificant rope attached to a halter, on a huge woolly head. Round and round the ring they go to be judged on the animal, then on themselves. She carries a shiny stick with a little hook to encourage him to place his hooves where he looks his best.

What babies her steers become. She washes them, grooms them, and carefully weighs and measures their feed. It is of the highest quality. We laugh at her animals when they love grooming so much that their enormous heads twist back, the long tongue comes out in a licking imitation, in rhythm with the brush strokes on their shiny clean hide.

Calf birthing is beautiful but can get technical when a mother goes into distress, and the vet has to be called, sometimes in the middle of the night, to assist. When things have calmed down, we watch for the little one to suckle for the important colostrum, which he must have during his first hour of life.

Sometimes we have a bull, and since they are unpredictable, I don't feed him inside. The others, dairy and beef cattle alike, all come inside to a fragrant and warm barn with the original dairy stanchions where I milk three cows.

At other times we watch for cycling cows and call for the artificial insemination technician to impregnate the cow, ordering the semen of the bull we like.

Every year we must watch the forecast for good weather before beginning to cut hay. Then it is turned over and over to assist the drying process before baling, loading it on to the hay wagon and hauling it into the barn for winter feed.

It is a hard life. A life full of hard work, but it's a good life, too, and I am determined.

Squirming squealing baby piglets are carried by their back legs to their lovely private house filled with deep straw where they cower, cuddled tight together with nervous eyes peeping out until they get used to us.

Ducks paddle and dive in their deep pond all day but are locked inside their house, where they go on their own each night. They need protection from raccoons and owls.

Customers pick up duck and chicken eggs from the porch fridge. Cleaning eggs is not my favourite farm chore, but I am determined.

I am determined to give my small child a wholesome life.

A big part of the wholesome life is 4H. The kids do demonstrations, public speaking, record keeping, and participate in shows all over. Finally, they sell their precious animal at a stock auction at the PNE in Vancouver. There are lots of tears.

Friends ask how we part with our animals that we love so much.

My stock answer is always, "Do you eat meat?"

We have given these animals a luxurious, comfortable life with clean bedding, loving care, and lots of clean water and good food to eat ~ a life much preferable to commercial endeavours.

And a wholesome life for us, too, because I was determined.

CHAPTER THIRTY-ONE

Near-Death Experience

I didn't see bright lights. I didn't feel serene. My life didn't pass before my eyes and time didn't stand still. Time didn't allow for any of this. There was no time. This is my one near-death experience.

There is something I have desperately wanted all my life, and it is my own farm. I crave it. I think I need it.

Eventually, in 1980, we purchase a lovely farm with a one-hundred-year-old farmhouse and an expansive dairy barn. How wonderful it sounds inside this barn with the rain falling on the sloping metal roof, the cows cozy and warm tossing their hay and crunching their oats.

On this farm, I have great respect for the power and hidden danger of machinery, a respect that I have had for as long as I can remember. In fact, farm machinery safety is my prime consideration. We use machinery daily. We can't farm without it.

On our new farm, I haul side-delivery rakes, plow shares, discs, harrows and, yes, even the fully loaded fragrant manure spreader. Each piece of machinery is treated with serious reverence and caution.

~~~~~~~

My tractor driving history begins as I grow up when Dad instructs safety first, and I learn to drive at twelve years of age. I climb up onto the ancient old red Cub tractor. Even such a small tractor deserves great respect. Dad and I clear an entire field of broom during that first learning experience.

He is out behind me, wearing old leather gloves with the palms worn through. He's the chokerman at the far end of the shining heavy chain. He loops the chain around the tall broom stalk and shouts, "Go!"

I release the clutch. I'm young and proud. It is a good beginning.

It's safety first again when, at sixteen, I am given the opportunity to drive a larger tractor hauling a hay baler. I fall in love with baling.

I keep hands, clothing, and hair away from the power take off, visible as it revolves at high speed, taking power from the tractor engine to run the baler.

I apply for a job custom baling and spend the summer travelling the area, a farmer's field here, another one there. I am eagerly up early to begin every day. I smile endlessly that summer. I am happiest on a tractor.

There is something about the baler picking up of long rows of dry hay ~ something about the auger pulling the thickness in, plunging it, digesting it, and producing a product that is easier for a person to handle, that I just love.

Barring a baler breakdown, bale after bale drop like gifts without ribbons from the baler chute. A bale every few feet.

Trucks plow along behind with haying crew helpers striking out like sunbeams to pick up and carry each heavy bale to the wagon. Laughter and good-natured teasing ring back from the dense woods surrounding the hayfield. Sun, cowboy hats, and everyone drenched in rivers of sweat.

Groggy wedding-cake tiers of overloaded wagons lumber slowly, rocking and righting themselves, straight to the barn before the weather changes.

~~~~~~~

Today on our new farm, we hurry with chores. We have fed the pigs, milked the cows, collected the eggs, and let the beef cattle out of their barn stanchions to graze.

Today we have a big project ahead. We plan to drag logs out of the skunk-cabbage swamp over the bank at the edge of the driveway next to the railway track. It will be a heavy job, so I take the biggest tractor we have. The tires are almost as high as I am tall. In this big work-horse of a tractor, I sit "down-in" on the spring-loaded seat. Wide steel fenders rise up left and right. The fenders give a feeling of security.

Carefully, I back up this big throaty, rumbling tractor. I stop just short of the steep bank that slopes down and away. My husband, the chokerman, drags the long chain, stretching it out to the first log. It's looped twice around the end of the log then hooked securely to itself. At his signal, and when he steps away, I let out the clutch. The powerful tractor surges to haul out the log. One after the other, the pile of logs grows larger and larger throughout the day. Everything is working efficiently, and all goes well. Soon the job will be done.

Now we're close to finished, and the swamp is cleared out.

I have twisted around in the seat, holding tight to one of the high tractor fenders when, without warning, this tethered log, instead of coming straight out, digs into the bank. The tractor can no longer move forward, but the massive tires are still driving. The first indication that something is wrong is when the front of the tractor rears up, and it begins to fall over backward, starting to dump me off.

Flight or fight tells me first to jump. I am terrified, and without thinking, I do try to jump. I tear my leg open on the gear shift trying to get off before the crash and inevitable crush. But common sense prevails, and in a nanosecond, I swing back in to slam the clutch down, which stops the drive and brings the front of the tractor thundering back to the ground with a bounce, bounce, bounce from the weight.

I shut down the engine. We two young farmers are paralyzed. It is a bright sunny fall day, but we don't see it. The birds are probably singing, but we don't hear them.

The skunk cabbages stink, but we don't notice it.

Right now, we just need to breathe.

I am stunned and in pain from the tear that has gone through both blue jeans and leg, but I am not as white as the chokerman. He doesn't move, a farmer statue of stone, in shock.

Things happen fast with machinery. Things can go wrong quickly.

We walk back to the farmhouse to apply a thick padded bandage.

We take a break now and, with still-trembling hands wrapped around mugs of hot steaming tea, discuss "what could have been," just grateful we'll both farm another day.

On this tractor, there is no roll-over bar, something I had given no forethought to ~ until the end of this day, the end of this experience. We study this thought and give it serious consideration.

CHAPTER THIRTY-TWO

Protector

I want to help and protect, but I must not if I am to raise a child to be independent.

It's a stifling hot September day, with dust motes in the air where the sun streaks in through the high windows. We sit on the top level of the bleachers at the Pacific National Exhibition (PNE), watching steers being led into the show ring one after the other to be auctioned off.

After the bidding, the auctioneer calls, "Going, going, gone!" for each one.

I am alarmed when I notice someone charging up the tiers of seating two at a time. Shockingly, it is to us he calls out.

"Come quickly! Your daughter has been hurt."

~~~~~~~

My child's father says I am a grizzly bear mother. I don't know how it came over me. I just grew long teeth and sharp claws of protection when my child was born. It was a rushing river of love.

We have a farm, and at nine years old, our daughter asks for a horse.

"Horses are expensive," I explain. "What about a steer? That way, you can make money."

And with that, she joins the local 4-H Beef Club. Soon we visit breeding farms to find the perfect "little" steer for her.

A "little" steer is awfully furry and pretty cute, but exceedingly strong. She spends long, arduous hours with him, working hard to tame the wildness out of him. He hates the halter and rope. He hates restriction. He twists and turns in circles of rebellion. He hops like a rabbit, and sometimes he flips himself completely over and falls right down on his side.

I want to help and protect, but I don't interfere. Training is a big adventure. That "little" steer tows my little girl around for weeks before she finally has him trained to follow her instead.

Eventually, he understands that she is the master, and she can lead him with a short length of rope clipped to his heavy leather halter with the white stitching. I have somehow restrained myself and haven't helped. She is remarkably tough and determined for a small girl.

He learns that she feeds him good oats that smell like the sugary molasses that she drizzles on them. There are sheaves of fragrant and tender green alfalfa hay. It smells so delicious that I sometimes want to taste it myself. Feed makes him eternally willing to come into the stanchion inside the barn at feeding time. There is a long line of stanchions, but he always chooses the same one. He thinks this is the only place to find his food, and he never makes a mistake.

He is washed with buckets of sudsy warm water with his own special soap, rinsed carefully, and brushed down, so shiny and sleek. His little mistress is soaking wet, too.

Careful records are kept of his special feed program since they must be handed in to the 4-H leader. Every bit of his feed is weighed on the shiny silver scale. This "little" steer grows rapidly on his good feed, soon becoming a thousand-pound steer, and even though she looks so small beside him, he is well trained now and easy to handle.

Mother-me would like to help, but she needs to do all the work herself.

Now it is time to show him. He is nervous about the stock rack on the back of the truck, and she has a bit of a rodeo on her hands until she can coax him inside. We travel to all the local fairs, and she enters classes on the steer himself, as well as classes for the showmanship of the handler.

Many months have passed, all leading toward the grand event, the PNE auction in Vancouver, where all 4-H steers will be sold to big buyers like Safeway and Thrifty's.

It is a huge emotional event for 4-H-ers since every kid has become extremely close to their pampered animal. Many tears are shed. These poor red-eyed kids try to get ready to part with their precious animal at the big auction. They will travel home alone, the stock rack sadly empty.

In the barns, we see kids cuddled up to their animals, in the deep clean straw, heads resting on their animal's belly, a dreamy look in their eyes, as these huge animals are lying down to rest and chew their cud.

There are rows of bright ribbons, like Butchart Garden flowers. Red, white, and blue proudly displayed on the wall above the string of animals in each club.

These kids are tremendously proud of their animals and love to answer questions from the fair-goers who come to see them.

This is a time of independence from parents as the 4-H leaders oversee the kids, and the kids themselves have many responsibilities. They lug bucket upon bucket of water to each animal in black rubber pails. They keep their animals immaculate by cleaning the straw during their assigned hours of stall duty.

I want to help and protect but nervous, protective mothers are not usually in attendance. All is organized and seems to go well until ~

Suddenly, we are shocked and running behind this messenger that has sprinted up the bleachers. OMG, what has happened? He explains as we run that our daughter has been kicked in the head by someone else's steer. We run. We run around buildings. We run around Playland rides. We run around crowds of people, unable to get to her fast enough.

It takes an interminably long time, the longest run of my entire life, to get to the St. John's Ambulance First Aid building where she has been taken.

We crash through the front door but are stopped immediately.

"You cannot see her!"

"Cannot see her?" I cry out. "OF COURSE I CAN SEE HER!"

"NO!" the authorities insist, someone thrusting a restraining arm in front of me.

"The doctors are checking her vital signs, and you cannot go in."

Right about then, I am ready to smash through the doors behind which my child is, without even opening them, making a person-outlined hole right through the wood. Fortunately, a doctor comes out at that very moment, to tell us we can come in now.

Michelle, poor little creature, looks bewildered and limp, just lying there on the gurney drained and white, but she is not crying. Not a single tear. I speak softly to her. Her cowboy boots have been pulled off. I massage her sock feet. After a couple of hours of observation, she seems to be okay, but we are told to take her directly to the hospital. There is another long observation period there, before the doctors clear her, warning us that if she starts to bleed out of her eyes or nose to rush her back.

None of this happens. She is tough, and she is okay.

~~~~~~~

I have always known how protective I am of her. I know exactly how much.

I still feel that way, though now she's 45 and doesn't need me. It seems she never did need me much.

CHAPTER THIRTY-THREE

Allergy

Today I am returning home from picking up a load of feed from Buckerfield's ~ forty sacks of poultry, beef and swine feed. My old jalopy truck rattles into our farmyard compound with clouds of dust rising on this hot summer day.

As I swing around to back into the barn, my husband comes up to the open window of the truck and says, "You might want to check on the kid. She has been stung by a bee and is not feeling well."

I reef the truck door open. I run, terrified. My child, my child!

I shout for her as I run through the door into our farmhouse. There is an eerie silence when my voice echoes. There is no answer. I race from room to room through the house, petrified, and finally find her, crumpled in a heap, on the floor, unconscious. How long has she been like this?

We purchased this farm with the intention of a good, healthy lifestyle. Everything has gone well so far, but now, what's happened?

I pick her up. Her nose is grossly swollen, many times its normal size. Her eyes are swollen shut, and red hives cover every part of her body that I can see.

I clutch her to me as I one-handedly dial the doctor who is, fortunately, nearby. I begin to explain to the nurse.

She interrupts. "Bring her here. Bring her here ~ quickly."

I try to give more symptoms, but she again interrupts. "Bring her here as fast as you can."

I scream for her father, and we fly out the long driveway. As we speed, I cradle her, but she is limp against me, and I am more terrified than I have ever been in my life.

A short distance from the clinic, she slowly comes around. I gather her up and run into the doctor's office. He is instantly there to check her vitals. Now that she is conscious, no adrenaline is required.

They keep us there at the doctor's office for over two hours, observing her to be sure she is safe. The nurse speaks to her softly and brings storybooks. I read them to her over and over. At last, we are cleared to take her home.

At home, I tuck her into her little bed, pulling her peach coloured quilt up to her chin. She clutches her "Elly" elephant for comfort. I read her endless stories, afraid to leave her. She is subdued, totally exhausted.

The following day, in his office, her doctor explains that she has had an anaphylactic allergic reaction, a life-threatening allergy to bee stings. We must take her immediately to an allergist. He chooses one in Vancouver.

At first, I don't understand this severe reaction because she has been stung before.

The doctor gently explains that the body will tolerate just so much, then suddenly it says, "No more."

Then, a long process begins.

Very soon, we travel by ferry for our appointment in Vancouver. She is only nine years old, and this will be an unpleasant experience for her. I wrack my brain to see how I can lessen the impact of the events I know are coming on this trip.

She sits between us ~ small, skinny, and apprehensive. Oh, how I wish I didn't have to put her through this.

I have a small, brightly coloured tin chest, all silver and blue. It has a domed lid and is used to hold toffee. There is a little lock on the front of the clasp and a key.

"Your treasure chest is filled with presents," I tell her.

I have individually wrapped and stuffed the little box with new-to-her small trinkets ~ an eraser, some miniature toys, a tiny ball, little games, a pencil, and tiny boxes of raisins.

"You can unlock the chest once every hour we are away," I say. "Take out one gift every hour."

Though she is quiet with anticipation and fear, the little tin of surprises does work to take her mind off the testing procedure, at least a little.

Nervously, we visit the allergist. They dress her in a flowery blue smock, opening at the back. The nurse marks her entire upper back into a mass of grid lines, so many squares. Bee venom of every kind is injected into each of the squares at timed intervals. They determine her allergy is to yellowjackets, a very aggressive wasp.

My tiny girl is crying, tired, sore, and clinging to me by the end of this procedure.

Then we sit across the desk for the consult with the allergist. He explains the next step. She will be desensitized in the hospital with an injection of yellowjacket venom, beginning at one part per million and working gradually up to the full amount of a sting. This technique is performed only in the emergency department of a hospital in case she has another allergic reaction.

In the meantime, her doctor and I must visit her school. The doctor will instruct the teaching staff on how to administer adrenaline with a needle from an AnaKit. They gather round the staff room to learn about this allergy and then make injections into an orange to get a feel for it and how to do the procedure correctly and thoroughly.

There are changes to make. No fragrant soaps. Be very careful with food. If a bee approaches, no flailing of arms. Just sit perfectly still until it leaves.

Now she and her friends always play at our house, nowhere else, since we are required to be with her.

A bustling, busy emergency department is not a place we enjoy. Still, we become friends with the staff because we're there through many weeks and months of increasing dosages of the venom until she can tolerate the amount of an actual sting.

She is in 4-H to show her beef cattle. When the kids are walking around the show ring in a line for judging, her club is resplendently represented by a uniform of blue jeans and red checkered shirts. She is unhappy that she cannot wear those colours, but yellow jackets like bright colours.

She says, "Awww, Mom, do I really have to?"

We must avoid the possibility of another sting while going through the desensitizing procedure by dressing her in all white clothing. She doesn't like that, not wanting to be different, and neither do we, but there is no choice. We have been warned.

The medical profession is doing its best to protect her, and we must, too.

There's no cotton candy at the fair either because yellowjackets like it better than she does.

We also carry an EpiPen of epinephrine and make sure one of us is always with her should she be stung and require it to be administered with a stab, even through clothing, into her thigh.

When the desensitizing program finally proves that she can tolerate a sting, our little family celebrates. The terrible ordeal is over, and she can return to a normal life, and her parents can breathe again.

CHAPTER THIRTY-FOUR

Locomotive Love

It's 1980, and we've just bought an old dairy farm in Nanoose Bay.

Along the entire back property line of the farm runs the railway. A freight train runs past twice a day. It runs up in the morning and comes back at the end of the day. And that's about all the thought I give to it.

On the day we move in with a convoy of trucks loaded with our belongings, our eight-year-old daughter, Michelle, hears the train approaching. She runs to me. She's dressed in her bib-front overalls. She's very excited about this new farming adventure. She tugs at my hand.

"Can we go see the train, Mommy?"

So we run across the field and wait behind the wire fence at the top of the bank. The train will pass just a few feet below, but very close to us ~ almost close enough to touch.

We make enthusiastic waves back and forth, and when they see us, they sound the locomotive whistle ~ toot, toot, toot-toot.

The cars clickity-click their way past. The brakeman in the caboose gives us a big wave, as well.

This small child is thrilled. It's easy to tell by the way she skip-hops back to the "new-to-us" but actually one-hundred-year-old farmhouse.

At the end of a long day of unpacking and setting up, she hears the train returning and pleads for us to watch again. They are on a downhill run this time, and they are flying. Sparks shoot from the wheels. The weight and the speed shakes the earth beneath our feet. They seem to know we would be waiting for them, as they're hanging out the windows this time.

Thus begins her happiness with all things concerning that train. She absolutely loves it. She runs out early mornings with lots of messy hair while she's still dressed in her jammies.

She runs out past her bedtime, signalling with her insignificant little flashlight.

Her farm chores are put on hold to run to meet her train.

One day the train slows at our farm. This has never happened before. As the locomotive slowly passes, the engineer has a big grin.

He calls out to her, "This is for you," and he throws something off.

It seems a long wait until the entire train passes that day, but at last, it is safe, and we race down the long driveway then back along the tracks to see what could be there.

We search in every direction through the long grass. Eventually, she finds it on her own. It is a lantern. It's a real lantern. This is what the engineer and brakemen use to signal to one another. It's big with a very powerful light. It's bright orange with a big looping handle over the top. Apparently, it's strong, too, because it has survived a very hard ground-landing completely intact.

Now there is no more insignificant little flashlight. Now she swings this official new lantern back and forth for the trainmen.

Later the train slows again. Once more, something is thrown off. This time it's a fresh battery for the lantern.

Another day the engineer sails through the air a train engineer hat ~ a real one, in stripes of blue and white.

Now when she hears the train coming, she quickly tugs on the cap over her braids, grabs her lantern, and runs to wave.

One day the train is coming up much slower than usual. Much slower. At first, we think there must be an animal on the tracks, but we see nothing. Then we think it must be an extremely heavy load because it is almost stopped. And then it is stopped, right there in front of us. This huge engine is huffing and puffing. It seethes with rumbling power.

The engineer calls out to me this time, with a big smile, "Can she come for a ride?"

Oh! We run back down the driveway and along the tracks to where that enormous locomotive waits for her. I stand beside the engine and lift her. The engineer pulls her up, up, up into that massive package of steel.

"Pick her up in Parksville," he calls with a big smile.

Now I stand alone as 32 cars pass by me. Almost every one is a rusty red boxcar with CN white lettering, some with scribbled graffiti, some empty flat decks and a few round oil tankers.

I watch as they cross the bridge over the river.

I watch the caboose. It gets smaller and smaller and smaller. I strain to watch until it disappears around the last bend into the forest. Then it is gone ~ GONE.

I am a little stunned.

It suddenly dawns on me, "Oh my god, my child is on that train."

But there's no time to worry. Quickly I jump into our farm truck. Dust billows as I fly down the driveway because I will race the train on its tracks with my truck on the highway.

I do make it before them, and as I wait and pace on the greasy old platform, I have time then to think then about how very good they have been to this child.

Finally, they thunder into the station with screeching steel wheels, that eventually stop that heavyweight hulk. I can feel that I am holding my breath a little, but then I see her with the engineer holding her shoulders from behind as he carefully steers her along the narrow catwalk on the side of that behemoth locomotive.

Both of them look delighted. Michelle is totally enchanted. Her eyes are just sparkling with excitement. We learn that this engineer's name is Norm. Now, she loves her train, and she loves the trainmen, but is it any wonder that Norm becomes her favourite engineer after this wonderful experience?

Life and a few years go by before ~

The train stops at our farm a second time. We don't know why. Incredibly, this time the engineer gets right out. He climbs up the steep bank to the fence where we are standing in the field. But he looks awfully sad.

He kneels down to speak softly to my daughter. He says he is sorry to have to tell her that Norm has unexpectedly died.

When we realize that we will no longer see Norm, heartbroken tears roll down our cheeks.

Then, he reaches through the fence and lifts up her hand. In it, he lays a tiny box.

"This is in memory of Norm," he says.

Slowly, she lifts the lid and there, nestled in cotton batten, is a beautiful little silver charm bracelet. There are tiny silver locomotives, railroad cars, and caboose all the way around.

Yes, there are many tender moments. These are big, strong trainmen, but they have made themselves an exceedingly extraordinary influence in a small child's life.

And I've learned a valuable lesson in humanity. This is much, much more than a freight train going by twice a day. I know these men now, and they fill me with awe and respect.

And maybe, just maybe, she makes their lives special, too.

Like on the night she hears them on their downhill run, heading for home. She races out across the snowy field. She carries a live fir tree, almost as big as she is. It is decorated with piles of tinsel and brightly coloured red and green decorations, a star, and it's beautiful. She has decorated this tree all by herself.

She lifts her tree up and waves it back and forth in arcs over her head.

This tree is just for them ~ a special tree to bring them home safely as they make their way to their families.

On a dark night ~

On this ~

Christmas Eve.

CHAPTER THIRTY-FIVE

I Don't WANT to Quit

Have you ever quit your job? Quit your job to move to a better job? This makes perfect sense. But we have not all quit jobs without a new job to replace it. For me, my psyche is screaming. I don't WANT to quit my job!

Working in a resort for 16 years, I have seen a lot. I've heard a lot. I've experienced a lot. Managing the office of a huge top-rated log cottage resort, at times, I think, "Now I've seen it all!"

This exceptionally exquisite resort is a continually expanding endeavour.

As a fledgling, I make reservations in a massive three-foot by two-foot ledger, using a pencil and an eraser. Arriving guests clomp and thump across a plywood lobby floor, leaving footprints behind on rainy and snowy days, cross to the insignificant little chipped office desk on which stands a single-line telephone. It's my job to both answer that phone and check-in guests at the same time. It was one employee at a time in those days.

At first, when I am a new employee, I am scared to be left alone in this cavernous log cave ~ especially at night, with nothing covering the windows, just me and the blazing lights within. The resort grows. As we grow, we double, then triple our staff working together. Over the prosperity of years, we move, not always gracefully, to computers, the paper ledger becomes extinct. Eventually, there is a soft-carpeted burgundy and brass-appointed classy and sophisticated lobby we are proud to offer to our guests.

There are over one hundred accommodation units now ~ private cottages, a lodge, and ocean view condos, all in stunning log construction. We add a massive indoor pool, an elegant log dining room, a spacious conference centre with many meeting rooms, and then a world-class spa.

Every day is exciting. We often run at 100% occupancy. Everyone wants to stay here.

There are incredible experiences here. I manage the office and customer complaints and, popular as this establishment is, there are many.

The boss tends to flare up and throw things, so, in the firm belief that this is not acceptable behaviour, I volunteer to take over. Happily, this position falls to me, but I thrive, and when I can make people happy again, I am completely fulfilled. I love this job.

Guests are always interesting. For instance, there is the man from Ontario who arrives with a chip on his shoulder and finds fault when there is none. I discover the hidden source of his feelings in our discussion when the door of my office closes. He tells me that he knows we in the west don't like anyone from the east. What?

I swear to him this is not true, and I have never heard such a thing. He is comforted then and, after our talk, stays for his vacation with satisfaction and joy. I know this because he comes back in to tell me and thank me.

On a routine day, I am talking on the phone when suddenly there is an earthquake. We work in a large log structure, and with logs moving, we think it prudent to run outside. I put my phone down on my desk without hanging up before my escape. Incredibly, the man is still on the phone when I return to my desk. I apologize profusely and begin to explain the reason for leaving our conversation. He explains that he felt the earthquake too. He lives in Vancouver ~ forty miles away. We agree ~ how amazing!

Immediately following the earthquake, one of my staff asks if he can transfer a call to me from the guest in 312A. She is not at all happy. Through my glass window, I noticed this young lady when she was checking in earlier, carrying a tiny infant.

Her first words are, "My room was shaking,"

I explain, "Yes, that is because we had an earthquake."

I am shocked when the next thing she says is, "Well, can you tell me if there will be more shaking, and when it will happen?" Now, again, I think I've heard it all.

Then there is a man from back east calling to book a reservation. I can tell he is not from anywhere near an ocean when he says, "The last time I stayed with you, the tide came in five miles."

"Actually, it's less than a mile, but it is incredibly beautiful on such an expanse of sand, isn't it?"

"Tell me, do you still participate in the tides?" he asks.

As non-plussed as I am, I gently explain. "Well, as long as we have a moon, we plan to participate in the tides, yes."

Sadly, this was not a joke. He meant it.

And, then there's the lady who is furious that a squirrel has dropped three pine cones on her vehicle.

"Give me compensation," she demands.

Again, it is not a joke.

One day I go out to help with check-in. Because we live on an island, the lobby is likely to be lined up about an hour after a ferry has disembarked, so it's all hands on deck to ensure an efficient check-in. Soon almost everyone has signed in and departed with their keys. Only Barry (of course, it has to be one of the men) and I are left at the front to welcome the two remaining arrivals.

The lady I am checking in leans way over our high front desk and whispers to me secretively, "I don't know if you've intended it, but your slip is around your ankles."

Oh no! I make a mad dash around the corner to hike back up this unfortunate slip with the broken elastic.

Registered guest names in a hotel can often be a problem, and we had our share of them. I once read a story about a man who made a reservation and explained to the clerk that his name is Stephens with a "PH." When he arrived, his reservation could not immediately be found under "S." Eventually, it was found ~ under "P" for "P-H-E-V-E-N-S."

A perk of having people skills is I get to travel a lot with my boss to promote the resort. She books us into swanky hotels because we get a preferred industry rate. I have never experienced glass-fronted hotels with gleaming wide open escalators that swish up two entire floors from the lobby, with their massive pool on the 17th floor.

It is a magnificent place to return to after working twelve hours on our feet, promoting our resort in a luxurious conference setting or the Seattle Kingdome. At night we sit exhausted on our beds eating Hagen Daz ice cream with plastic spoons knowing there's another tough day ahead of us tomorrow just the same as this one.

It took me a while to understand that, even though I might recognize a guest checking in, it is best not to acknowledge that I do. This is a hotel, after all.

One day I check in a doctor from France. As he leaves with his key, he stands aside for a man coming in through the door. Each of them stops in their tracks. Suddenly, they are in an emotional embrace with back-patting and emphatic exclamations of joy. At last, they part, joyfully agreeing to meet in the lounge in an hour. Fortunately, I can check-in the second man. It turns out he is a doctor as well. But this doctor is from Australia, and I was able to glean the story.

These two had trained together in medical school and had not seen one another since. On a resort as large as ours, if they had not met when and where they did, they most likely would not even have crossed paths. One told me on departure two weeks later that their meeting here, when they live on different continents, was a miracle and that they had shared a wonderful reunion.

There are thousands of resort tales like these.

~~~~~~~

So, there I am, stimulated and enchanted with my long-time position, not wanting to quit.

But there is someone and something very important in my life. A new love in my life. This significant love and the source of my happiness is Phil. Phil has weekends off. I do not ~ at least not many.

Because I have people skills, my employers would like to have me there 24/7, but I need more weekends off because of this newfound happiness and my relationship with my wonderful, beautiful Phil. However, they are not willing to budge on this issue. I respect and fully understand their point of view, but I cannot live with it now. So, with deep unhappiness, I quit.

I am devastated. My beloved job is gone, but it is my choice. Whatever will I do now?

CHAPTER THIRTY-SIX

But, Can I Do It?

This sad evening, I punch in my daughter's phone number hesitantly.

"Hello, honey, it's Mom. I want to tell you before you hear from someone else, I quit my job today. I won't be going back."

Instead of being shocked or distressed, she says with joy and enthusiasm, "Great!"

I am not expecting that reaction.

"We're looking for weeders," she says.

She is a foreman in a Landscaping Horticulturist position.

She quickly says before I have time to protest, "Let me phone my boss to see if I can hire you. I'll call you right back."

Click. Click? Oh no!

Beads of sweat start on my brow. It actually trickles. I am a 52-year-old office worker who has spent her entire career behind a desk. My shoulders slump. I slink onto the couch. I lay flat. I try to keep calm. I try to keep breathing, at least.

But all I can think is, "Can I keep up with those youngsters? Can I keep up, more accurately, with her? What if I can't do it? What if we work for the same company and I let her down?"

I bound back up from the couch in a panic when she instantly phones back.

"You start at 7 a.m. tomorrow!"

To her, I say, "Great! Thank you. Whatever you do, don't call me Mom at work. Just my first name, please."

To myself, I say, "I can't do it. I know I can't do it. What a nightmare."

Everyone in my new environment is very welcoming, fun-loving, and friendly ~ maybe a little bit crazy and slightly skeptical about this new older employee, but great. The boss is, understandably, a little more serious. I am thirty years older than everyone else.

I have known a lifetime of gardening but never anything commercial. Commercial gardening is entirely different. Speed is everything. Remember the seriousness of the boss? Efficiency is key.

I help to load trucks and trailers with power tools, fuel, and equipment, and we blast out the long driveway in a convoy of trucks. Trucks with workers, trucks with tools, trucks with bobcats, ladders, and wheelbarrows.

The law is laid down by my foreman, my daughter. I am determined to prove myself. I sweat honest sweat, lots of it, with no time to wipe it out of my eyes. I work my fingers to the bone.

Miss Foreman is a tough taskmaster, instructing, "The most important thing is to remove the root of each weed. No slicing or breaking it off because it will only grow back if you do."

I am to use a strong pronger to loosen the soil, only in small patches, not getting ahead of myself, but working very quickly. I am but a lowly weeder, but she informs me that my work will be inspected. I work so heads-down-hard, I am shocked when break time arrives, followed by lunch and quickly by another break. It is with great relief that my work passes the foreman's inspection.

I thrive in this environment and eagerly set out on each new workday adventure one after another, all of it stimulating and unique. I learn to use a power hedge trimmer with a long ferocious bar of gnashing flying cutters that become a blur at full power. One little slip and that blur will cut through blue jeans into a leg ~ my leg. I tell no one, but I wear fallers' pants after that.

Commercial landscaping means speed, so you'd better learn quickly to work fast. For me, it means continually proving myself because of my age, but I grow strong rapidly and now need a belt to hold up my jeans. I blossom as I learn all these new skills.

Every morning I pack my duffel bag. Four litres of water, lunch for a logger, as we need good fuel for our bodies. Now, add the smaller tools, knee pads, and rain gear because we work a lot in the rain. Stuff in the reflective big-"X" safety vest and I am off.

~~~~~~~

When my daughter no longer works for the company, I move up in rank with a crew of my own and a dump truck that I love.

Working for the city, we are exceptionally well paid, even for garbage pick-up, which is an occasional part of the routine, and a duty I love because it gives me lots of time to think and plan.

We often need to lay entire fields of sod. Trailers stacked high with freshly cut rolls of heavy sod lying on wooden pallets, waiting to be unloaded. As we haul them from the stack, we stagger like drunks under the weight. Even the male workmates can't carry more than one. It's the most demanding work of all. And then, it takes finesse when we lay the turf down ~ each must be fitted perfectly, so the joins don't show.

There's dangerous work to be done in roadside medians ~ dangerous in a couple of ways. First, because of the traffic and second, because of the danger of lurking hypodermic needles. I carry a sharps disposal unit under the seat of my truck. In a city park remediation project, I find 21 needles in 3 days. This is scary. It is always the first caution I give to new staff.

We do all the work the men do. I often have all-female crews, and it is truly amazing what we can accomplish.

It is essential to have my crew comfortable with my driving. One day upon arriving at a far away worksite, we stand and stare at the back bumper of the truck. One of the crew had placed her coffee cup there before we left the shop. It is not only still there, but it's still full too.

I once weeded right up to a duck sitting on a clutch of eggs. She waited until I was just about right over the top of her before she raised an hysterical squawk and flapped into my face before frantically winging away. My heart nearly stopped.

One day I have to haul a bobcat on a trailer for the first time. Brett's instructions are alarming.

"Make sure you slow down well ahead of stopping. If you don't, the weight of the trailer will push you right through the intersection."

Grateful for that information, I proceed with great care.

Every day I love to go to work. It is sure to be an adventure. I feel so fortunate and wish I had always worked in this industry!

Working on a rose garden one day, my workmate, Jade, whispers to me, "Don't look now, but there's someone living in the canoe."

In this park, there is a beautifully carved and colourful Native canoe, all red and blue and yellow. It's mounted high up under a roof to protect it from the weather. I bide my time then sneak a peek. I see a homeless man struggling to open a can of soup. Later I call the boss. He's not at all sure he believes me, asking if this is legitimate.

I say, "Absolutely, go ahead and report it."

I am a bit sad, though, as my mind goes to how cozy he must be up there in his little canoe-nest. I picture a sleeping bag in the bow and a stash of his meagre belongings in the stern. How resourceful he is.

I find myself working alone one day, on gardens surrounding an enormous round cement water-supply tank, for which I will gain access with a city key. There is a substantial steel gate with an enormous dangling padlock ~ a padlock that is rusty and won't unlock. I am in the middle of nowhere.

"Figure this out, kid, I say to myself. Nobody is going to do this for you."

Then I get a brainwave! I open the hood of my truck, pull out the oil dipstick and run it to the lock. I let the oil drops fall into the lock. After a few trips running back and forth, it works, and I'm in!

Working near the ferry terminal on December 24th, my partner, Sonja, and I are slaving. It is gushing rain from a leaden, dark grey sky. We're in heavy steel-toe work boots, bulky yellow bib-front pants. Jackets with hoods tightened around our wind-blown faces. A big "X" safety vest is over top of everything. The headlights of a steady stream of vehicles headed for the ferry trying to make it home for Christmas are reflecting on the flooded streets. Rooster tails from whirling tires continually splash us.

Suddenly, we hear the choked words of the boss calling to us over the noise of the speeding traffic. "What are you girls still doing out in this? The rest of the crew went home hours ago." We high-five. We are so dedicated!

In this industry, I learn a lot about "the other side of life." We use the big steel boxes the size of railroad boxcars, loading them with debris and branches. I am warned to check carefully each morning when I swing the massive steel box door open, in case people are sleeping inside.

Then one day, a little emergency ~ SLAM! UH OH!

My hands fly up to grab my head. Oh no, if I could only take this moment back. I have just locked my keys inside my work truck. The window is down just a little bit. I don't want to have to call my boss, Brent, to bail me out, hoping to deal with this situation myself. So I knock on the door of the nearest house. The male occupant that opens the door only a crack, doesn't smile, and looks at me very suspiciously when I explain the problem.

"Hi," I say, "I've locked the keys in my work truck, and I need a coat hanger."

He looks at me as if he doesn't trust me one bit, but he does come out with a coat hanger, and together he and I break-in. There's the company logo on the side of the truck door, and he has a good description of me.

I say enthusiastically, "Thank you. You really saved the day."

Imagine my shock when he turns as he is striding away and laughingly calls over his shoulder, "Say hi to Brent." It turns out he is good friends with my boss, who is going to hear about this, after all.

So, I more than work for this company. I am smitten with this work. I exude exuberance. Every day is a joy for me. I am beyond happy here and, hands down, I am the most enthusiastic employee.

Oh, and the belt? Well, it got tightened and tightened and tightened some more. Landscaping is hard work. But, oh, how I loved that job.

I thought no job could compare to the one I have just left, but my new job is the most challenging and best job I've ever had.

And I have every weekend off too!

CHAPTER THIRTY-SEVEN

Finding Lost Stones

People have feelings about cemeteries, and everyone feels differently. How do you feel? Is being in a graveyard a good experience for you or, well, maybe not so much?

I love cemeteries and spent many years working in them. I find a cemetery a peaceful, beautiful place with endless expanses of grass, a serene place I genuinely love to be.

But it didn't start that way for me.

Once upon a long time ago, I would not even enter a cemetery. No, thank you! One day in England with my family, I find myself in a graveyard, ostensibly to look for headstones of relatives.

Everyone else shuffles happily under the ancient weathered wooden arbour that guards the cemetery entrance. Sweetly fragrant white-rose vines drape thickly down in a tangle.

As everyone ducks under, I raise my hand and signal stop.

"Just leave me here," I say.

I shudder and cower behind. I have not, even once, been in a graveyard, and I am not about to start now.

As I sit hiding on the wooden bench outside waiting for them to return, I can see a work party hard at work just inside the arbour, right next to the quaint old stone church. I become more and more intrigued. Eventually, it becomes too much for me, and I do find the courage to enter this timeworn place.

I see an equally timeworn gentleman in a tweed Sherlock Holmes cap. The ear flaps are tied up at the top. He wears woollen knee-breeches and has stopped his work to wipe the sweat from his brow.

I approach him. "May I ask what is it you are doing here?"

The headstones are ancient and as tall as I am, with absolutely no inscriptions to be seen, smooth as river stones except for the purple topped, lacy flat lichen that grows on them. There is absolutely nothing to see as if there had never been words inscribed.

The old gentleman explains. "First, we gently scrub the headstones with clear water, no soap, using scrub brushes, then we..."

I listen to the sound of scrubbing, scritch, scritch and then stand entranced and amazed to see them hold a large sheet of aluminum as big as your dinner table at the perfect angle to reflect the day's extremely dim British sunshine onto the face of the stone. There, at last, the entire inscription is legible! Like a rabbit out of a hat, this is magic!

"Then," he continues, "we record the names, words, and dates in the book of records which is stored inside the church."

~~~~~~~

And so, long ago, that's how it all began.

I am now the foreman of my own landscaping crew.

We contract to the city, and this includes a lot of cemetery work. In these graveyards, we prune miles of hedges into perfect rectangles, weed beautifully designed and intricate gardens, and maintain headstones.

It is a fact that over time, headstones lean and tilt, and sometimes they can fall right over and sink into the soil. I haul truckloads of sand used to level all the stones. Thousands of stones. Each stone is pried up and lifted with great care and placed just above its location since we must return it to the exact same place where it was previously. Then sand is added to the lower side of the hole to make the stone level and lovely once again.

It is heavy work. The plastic face of my watch reflects many long scratches from the unfinished underside of the headstones. We spend long days levelling stones, holding the heavy weight up with one hand while smoothing the sand underneath.

That's what we do with visible stones.

~~~~~~~

But do you know? There is a secret below. There are stones beneath the surface. The older ones are as deep as a foot down. No one knows where they are. Part of what our team does is "finding stones." I call it "finding lost people."

You see, nature has a way of burying headstones. The wind blows leaves and soil into depressions, grass grows in and around, and the stones become lost, sometimes for many long decades.

We are hired to find them and raise them to the surface.

The method we use is the most laborious work of all. We have a four-foot-long round steel rod. Sharply pointed on one end, it is very thick and extremely heavy. We raise it high overhead as if spearing for fish and thrust with extreme force into the ground. You want it to go a long way down.

If you feel a great thud and your back teeth are knocked loose, that's a headstone. Well, at least it is nearly always a headstone. Occasionally, it can be a rock. Then the digging begins.

It is the most exciting thing you can imagine to dig down to a headstone and bring it up to the surface. We cry out in triumph, and everyone comes to have a look.

"Come here! Come see this one!"

Some of these magnificent stones are extremely old. The older they are, the better we like it. There are stones of all different shapes and sizes and inscriptions and sad, tiny ones for babies.

It is a good day when we find eight or ten. An excellent day and the best we ever had was finding 27 stones and bringing them all to the surface.

Then the hole is filled, and the new stone is placed correctly and ceremoniously on the surface, now in its rightful place, radiant. It is a great reward.

Now family and genealogy researchers can find the stones they are looking for, like my family and I did back in England that day.

One day I spot a city employee I know who is labouring. Usually, it is just us working there, so I walk down to ask him what he is doing. He says he is digging to make a place to put an urn of ashes there. I am stunned because he is alone, just him.

"But there is no one here," I say. "Where are her people?"

"She has no people," he says sadly.

~~~~~~~

At day's end, I return the crew to the shop, put a truckload of tools away, and call out, "Have a good evening," to each.

But, even though it's been a tough day and I am weary, I do not head west for the long drive home this day.

I turn and head back into town. Then I return to the cemetery, to the lady's urn. I place a bouquet of white lilies beside her.

I make a little speech. I tell her, "You're not alone. I am here with you. I care about you. I hope you had a good and happy life."

I crouch there and linger for a long time.

Eventually, I straighten up and pull myself away.

All the lonely people,
Where do they all come from?
All the lonely people,
Where do they all belong?

Slowly, slowly, the steel-toed work boots walk away.

CHAPTER THIRTY-EIGHT

First Flight to the USA

We all have significant challenges, right? Challenges that we think we may not be able to realize? This one puts sweat on my brow. It fills me with anxiety and a dry mouth ~ like when a traffic cop gives you a ticket. This was one of the biggest challenges of my life.

As we do every year, we are leaving for the colossal Arlington Airshow in Washinton. Traditionally, we take Phil's large vintage Harvard aircraft, a showpiece.

But I have a puffed-up pigeon chest of pride in my shiny new airplane. Actually, it is very old. I want to take my little one this time so that I can fly. My plane, like me, has probably never experienced USA flight either.

I am anxious to achieve this flight myself. I sweat about it for weeks ahead and continuously wonder if I can do it. I ponder it deeply in many a velvet nighttime, curled up to my big strong pilot husband.

It will be a complicated and highly technical landing procedure, this much I know.

I phone ahead to the Department of Transportation in Washington to ensure I understand all the safety and protocol procedures.

The woman I speak with is immensely helpful and cheerful but ends our conversation with a warning:

> *You must not overfly a congregation or gathering of people of any kind AND remember that if a jet should appear on your wing and the pilot points to the ground, he is motioning you to land immediately and if you do not comply he has the authority to shoot you out of the sky.*

This is not a joke.

"Yes, ma'am," I reply.

I take it as seriously as she meant it and worry a little more, but I am still determined. At least for the time being, I do not back out.

It's now early morning, and no one is around. Eagles fly overhead. Camping supplies ~ the pup tent, sleeping bag, food, toiletries, even the sunscreen ~ are gathered together and weighed carefully on a scale. Then we add the weight of our two souls.

My tiny airplane will not lift off if overloaded. Weight and balance of the load are equivalent to safety. We pare down the supplies, leaving non-essentials behind because we have to. Now we are 100% sure about weight.

Although I am confident about my capabilities, doubt has a way of creeping in. I self-talk.

The angel sitting on my shoulder interferes with a whisper, "You can do it, Lee, you know what you are doing." I remind her I have not flown in the USA before.

It is a sunny, hot summer morning, and we load the plane. The baggage is sitting on the tarmac, which is melting in the shimmering waves of heat, waiting to be stowed in the baggage compartment.

My stomach contains some multi-coloured fluttery butterflies now, but I push myself on.

~~~~~~~

OK, then, last chance. Everything is loaded and secured and tied down with rope in case we encounter turbulence. The airplane walk around is complete. The checklist is checked off. My flight plan is filed. I have forgotten nothing.

The windshield is polished to invisible perfection inside and out for even the tiniest speck would look like a bird in our flight path.

It is a momentous occasion in my life. I am lucky to have a way out, though, as I know Phil will willingly take over if I can't go through with this.

We swing and rattle the giant aluminum hangar doors. They close with an ominous clang. This is it.

Then comes the moment of truth. There is only one door into the cockpit. Whoever enters first will slide across the first seat onto the pilot's seat on the left, which is worn and patched with duck tape. There is still a moment to allow Phil to enter first. I look sideways at him. I think carefully. Should I? It would be so easy.

But, no, I make my decision. Hand on snowy white wing strut I step, now with confidence, onto the landing gear tire and swing myself up into the cockpit first. I am the captain. I am happily in control.

More detailed cockpit checks. Check, check, check. Then we secure ourselves into the three-point harnesses that snap with a reassuring click. I strap on my metal kneeboard and cinch its elastics. My map tucks under my leg for easy access.

Out the window, I shout, "Clear prop," then fire up. After an engine run-up and final instrument check, I taxi to position and take off.

The flight is lovely with the early morning sunshine on the coastal mountains. I report into air traffic control at all required points.

"Charlie Foxtrot Charlie Quebec Mike, level at 3,000 transiting the zone to Arlington Washington."

Everything goes as expected. As I cross the border, though, we both have our sharpest eagle eyes searching the ground below. Starboard, port and all-around scanning for any congregation, cluster, or crowd there may be below us. Is that a stadium? Is that a rally? With immense relief, we see no gatherings en route.

I plead with the spirits of flight that we have beat the rush, but then, dropping down and approaching to pattern altitude for landing, I encounter the most crowded airplane situation in which I have ever flown. I fit the plane in where I can. It is extremely congested. There isn't even elbow room. It's like flying in the Snowbirds aerobatic team. There is a blue Cessna on my left wing, a yellow Piper on my right. I am close behind the aircraft in front, and no doubt, there are many behind.

Speaking with the tower, aircraft for this event deviate from the norm of calling our aircraft call signs, and we give only our type and, importantly, our colour so they can keep us all organized.

"Green and white Tripacer," I say.

Uh, oh, now I hear there is another Tripacer behind, but fortunately, it's a different colour.

Normally aircraft land singularly, but there are so many in this incredible beehive of swarming aircraft that we each are instructed to land right, land left, or land center, and incredibly we land successively as rapidly as the tick-tick-tick of the second hand on a clock. Amazingly, and thank god for the skill of air traffic control, it turns out well. We triumphantly taxi to clear customs.

~~~~~~~

That night we sit happily beside our little army tent under the stars and under the wing of this great little airplane in the "antique" section of the flight line. I am satisfied with my achievement today. I held my own.

And I am smiling because no pilot needs a jet on the wing!

CHAPTER THIRTY-NINE

Little Brown Bear

"She's crying, Phil. Oh, how can we leave her when she's crying?"

We continue to drive away, aware that we will make things harder if we go back. I cry, too, because I can't bear to see our tiny granddaughter cry.

I wave from the motorhome window as we leave on a five-month trip across Canada. We have never been away from her for so long.

The tears, however, are not for Namma, and they're not for Poppa. They are for Little Brown Bear, her stuffie. He is not a special one. He is not more special than any of the other ones. She calls them "my favourite guys" and treats all her stuffies like people.

I look at her tiny face, and I wish, wish, wish her mother had not suggested we take Little Brown Bear across Canada with us.

At four years old, it is hard for her to understand that he will come back.

But now we're gone, and she'll soon forget. Perhaps Little Brown Bear will have adventure stories for her when he comes back.

We travel a long way north this first day, and he has adventure #1 straight away! It's May first. We are the only campers in this entire rugged campsite.

We step outside to Crunch! Crunch? Deep snow surrounds us, right up to Little Brown Bear's fuzzy knees. He's shivering, so we bring him back inside to warm up. He's not a polar bear, after all, just a chocolaty fuzzy little dude with pigeon toes and glassy eyes seemingly anxious to be on his way.

Shall we give it a try? Do we need chains?

Riding up front in the cab, he thinks it is a fine thing for a very small bear to jounce along.

We sing at the top of our lungs, "Adventuring We Will Go." And, we sing every morning when setting out, for we have a plan. Part of our heritage originates from Newfoundland, and we are determined to see it.

After many months of travelling, we are, at last, in Nova Scotia waiting excitedly for the long ferry ride to Newfoundland. As the colossal ferry docks, Little Brown Bear's nose is pressed to the porthole. He sees Newfoundland's iconic colourful red, blue, and yellow buildings, just as he knew he would.

In this grand adventure, his very favourite place so far is Newfoundland. We are related to the famous Arctic explorer, Captain Bob Bartlett, and a visit to his village of Brigus is our destination.

We discover Bob Bartlett's notoriety in his home town is extensive, with monuments and an old stone barn museum, filled to bursting with relics.

We walk through a dark tunnel heading for the pinpoint of bright light at the far end. This tunnel was blasted through solid rock on the waterfront of Brigus in 1860 to provide access to a deep water berth for Bob Bartlett's sailing ship.

As we wander through the Bartlett family home, Little Brown Bear is shocked to learn that Captain Bartlett once brought a live polar bear cub back from the Arctic. Quick, hurry back through the tunnel and sail that polar bear back as he becomes hungrier and hungrier!

We stop at the post office to send postcards, and we are surprised to be able to purchase Bob Bartlett stamps.

We see thousands of domed lobster traps piled high in leaning Eiffel towers, representing a Newfoundland industry. Along the highways, vegetable gardens miles from civilization make this small bear wonder how the scant two-foot-high fences could possibly keep out the abundant moose. Firewood hauling sleds are universal in this remoteness.

During our entire trip, Little Brown Bear meets no people more friendly than the Newfoundlanders. They offer us tea, lunch, handmade trinkets, help, and conversation. How they recognize us as being "from away" is a mystery, but they can tell easily, it seems.

Boat rides are not for small fuzzy bears, but it is a must to see the blue-white mountainous icebergs off Newfoundland. Many passengers eat iceberg-ice scooped out of the sea by a net.

Whales breech and spout all around this day, and flukes splash water toward us, seeming to send us on our way back home.

We return after our long journey to find our small grandchild bigger. We hug her tightly. There are no tears now.

Little Brown Bear is a worldly bear now. She laughs to see him again. She cuddles him and doesn't let him out of her sight for a long, long time.

CHAPTER FORTY

Nana Mac's Air

I want to go to Newfoundland. I've always wanted to go. I need to breathe the air that my grandmother breathed. Although she married Donald Steven McKinnon and we call her Nana Mac, her maiden name was Charlotte Kedel Lee. I am, and my cousin Richard Lee was named after her.

Part of my soul belongs to Newfoundland. This I've always known.

Can I go now? No ~ much too young.

Can I go now? No ~ my then-partner is not interested.

Why do I need so badly to go? I don't know, as my memories of her are not good.

Thinking back, I remember being terrified as Nana Mac reaches for the earpiece of the big wooden box telephone that hangs on the wall.

She tells the operator, "8438L1, please." When my mother answers, she yells into the phone, "Come and get her right now. She is touching my things."

I am maybe 3, but these words echo in my mind still and stab at my guilt. I still see her anger. She seems very old to me. Gray wispy hair halos her head. Grandmother is kindly except when she's not and mostly, she's not.

There are high-up windows in her tiny basement suite. I am scared of her and very small. I tip my head back to watch those far up windows. I see feet hurrying by, sloshing and slushing in rubber boots. I can't see the people-tops, but surely there are umbrellas. Am I watching for my mother?

Her one-room suite has a pull-out couch with lacy antimacassars. Is it these that I have touched?

This is my mother's mother, the same grandmother that my mother tells me, phones her on the day of exactly nine months after my parent's wedding, saying, "Okay, you can have the baby now." That baby is me, the first of the four kids my parents will eventually have.

Can I go to Newfoundland now? No, not now ~ I am a farmer. Animals can't be left.

Now? Now? Can I go now? No ~ too busy raising my child.

My entire life, I have wished to go to Newfoundland, feeling a yearningly strong pull.

Now? Can I go now?

Now there is Phil. The shiny newness of the happiest time of my life.

Phil lived in Manitoba until he was ten and has never been back. We have heard they are to close this company town of Pointe du Bois.

One day Phil says casually to me, "We should drive to Pointe. The demolition of the 44 buildings of the town will leave no trace ~ a ghost town. I would love to see it again before they bulldoze it. We can continue to Newfoundland where you have always wanted to go."

A smile crosses his face.

We plan, scheme, and arrange a five-month tenant for our house, and in 2010 we go. I want to look for "my people" in the cemetery. I want to feel the air, listen to the way people talk. I just need to be there. I want to see the brightly coloured houses. I want to breathe my grandmother's air.

I taste anticipation all those thousands of miles and months of driving.

Then, not so suddenly, we are here. In my mind's eye, I picture a quaint, tiny, and ancient cemetery. But instead ~ I stand at the St. John United Church cemetery gate. I stand on tippy toes to see the headstones in vast fields. Miles of lines. Miles and miles of rows. I am overwhelmed. They disappear over the hill. I can't see the end. So many ~ too many.

I abandon my lifelong quest to find my people. I inhale slowly and deeply. I breathe "her" air, Nana Mac's air. It is enough just to be here now. I know I have come. A warm and friendly blanket of satisfaction washes over me, and I am changed.

CHAPTER FORTY-ONE

She Does Only Fabulous

It is late. I stand in Emergency. She sleeps. As I stare horrified at the multitude of connections to monitors and watch her heart rate reflected in eerie green pulses ~ I reflect on her life.

She has just stepped off one of the biggest ships in the world after a journey across the Atlantic. Her breath is taken away by the beautiful department stores there. In this one, she gazes about in wonder until she discovers the youngest of her two children is missing. Store clerks are sent searching. Announcements echo from speakers. As a last resort, she rushes outside to glimpse the shirttails of this little three-year-old son departing down the street behind the drum of the marching band in a parade.

Then she, her husband, and two young children live in a tiny cabin on a hill in Departure Bay, Nanaimo ~ Sugar Loaf Mountain. There is one electrical outlet and no running water. Water is carried by the bucketful from a well on the backtrack. A third baby is born while they live here.

She is a dancer and actress at heart and teaches a line of little girls in short frilly costumes and tap shoes. She is crowned "Miss Departure Bay" even though she is a "Mrs." and a young and beautiful mother. She does only fabulous.

With this tiny new baby in her pram, she walks for miles to catch the bus to the city.

Real estate moguls have watched her for years and, seeing this long-legged beauty striding with such determination, one day, they knock on her door with a proposition. They want her to take the real estate course, learn to drive, and come to work for them. All of this, she does. She doesn't just sell houses and properties, she becomes a hugely successful agent, and she loves her work. She is known in the industry as "honesty itself." She does only fabulous.

She is retired now and lives in a facility with a stunning lake view. Today I kick off my shoes and pad softly across her white carpet. She has a warm plaid blanket across her knees. I sit at her feet, putting socks on for her ~ a job too difficult now ~ thinking about how she has been my mentor for my entire adult life.

Her lovely hair is tied close to the top and is adorned with a cluster of multi-coloured artificial flowers ~ red, yellow, blue. She does only fabulous. When the flowers are not in her hair, they are attached to the handles of her walker, ready for meeting her friends in the facility dining room.

She still has the ten-cent red and silver tin star that sat shining atop the Christmas tree every year. I cannot remember a time that it wasn't there, though she can well afford an expensive star now.

She has a firm belief in fairies.

"I saw them as a girl in England on Amberley Mount," she says.

Delicate flowers and leaves are pressed between pieces of waxed paper to make stunning tiny flower fairies. She publishes limited-edition books of these little fairies. Each one has been given a name ~ The Joystick Fairy, The Cobweb Fairy.

She loves Shirley Temple, and when her child was small, she hated to have her curly hair styled in a Shirley Temple likeness and being dressed in Shirley Temple clothes, all designed and hand made on a hand-crank sewing machine.

This lady, this grand and beautiful lady I speak of, is my 99-year old mother-in-law and, though I am no longer married to her son, she has kept me close. I am treated with great respect and abiding love, as I always have been.

~~~~~~~

Tonight machines continue to flash and beep, and my reverie is broken when suddenly, Mom's eyes flutter open. She is very sick.

She grasps my hand and says, "I hope I am taken soon."

I shudder.

"Oh, no, Mom ~ please don't say that. I need you here. Many of us need you here."

I know what I, what we all, want is unrealistic and unattainable.

My life has been and still is much happier for the presence of such a wonderful influential person of such wisdom.

Midge Rees, you have added such pleasure and richness to my life. I will be lost without you.

You truly do ONLY fabulous.

CHAPTER FORTY-TWO

The Dog Ate My Homework

I am always so sad if I ever have to miss my beloved writing class, but there is a job I have needed to do. A job that I have needed to do for 20 years! I hate to, but I cancel writing class. My teacher asks if the dog ate my homework.

~~~~~~~

Oh, Phil, what a lot of stuff. Regaining my health for three entire days after a long illness, I speak to myself.

"If I still feel good three days from now, I will tackle the near-impossible."

The three days pass. I am no longer sick. Well, to be honest, there are a lot of equilibrium issues, but I am determined to start. I am twenty years and three months behind.

The story begins with my sweetheart selling his farm. As the ink dries on the sale agreement, he realizes that all his farm possessions must come to our shed. It's a large shed, it's true, but there is a tremendous amount of stuff, all of which is packed like little farm sardines and what's leftover goes into our garage.

So much stuff, Phil, but neat as a pin, he puts things together like a jigsaw puzzle, so it all fits. Click, click. He wedges every piece together, not a squidge of space is wasted.

Walking into either structure feels like I should scrunch my shoulders together make myself narrow enough to pass through the dark tunnels of stuff.

Compounding this terrible job is the rat infestation in the shed. I knew they had moved in three months ago. I can hardly breathe for the stench. Everything soft enough for nests has been chewed so finely it looks like it has been through a grinder. They have shredded Christmas light strings, leaving only the bulbs lying sadly in piles of red and green.

I continue this horrible job because if I were to die, I would hate to leave this mess for my daughter to manage. So much stuff. It is truly unbelievable.

One by one, a million pieces I remove from that building. I make a long, wide row of things to go to the dump on the left of the long driveway and the few things I intend to keep in a little pile on the right, removing rat mess and nests as I go.

After two days of dawn to dusk dragging out and sorting, I call the junk removal man. We load two behemoth trucks. He, his helper, and I stack heaping loads between the high extended plywood sides. Ropes are zig-zagged across the open backs to hold it all in. They pull away and head to the junkyard with my thousand dollars in hand. The cost is so high because of the bricks, the wood, the asphalt shingles, all of which they must pay to dump.

Oh, Phil, so much stuff ~ none of which I ever need, nor will I ever use.

The next day I work some more ~ sorting and piling. I demolish an old structure at the back of my property. With powerful sledgehammer thwacks, I swing until the building lies in a pile of what looks like an iceberg. I cart it all to the front, load by load, on the wobbly wheelbarrow. Junk guy rumbles away with another Eiffel Tower of junk, this time with $900 of my puny wealth.

I don't tell him, as I am not sure I have the stamina for it, but my intention for the following day is to sort and throw away as much as possible of what is in our garage, much of it belonging to Phil's parents when we moved them in to live with us after Mom's stroke.

Junk guy can't believe I've called him again, but I do after the decisions have been made. This time he removes a gazillion construction bags I've filled, leaving for the final time with yet another fistful of green, but only $380 this time, seeming almost measly, but not quite.

Phil would be horrified at the cost of his "farm dispersal."

But I am lighter than air with it all gone even though my wallet is also lighter. Phil is worth it, for my life with this man was beautiful, wonderful, and the happiest I have ever been. Not a bit of our life together was junk.

CHAPTER FORTY-THREE

Blood Brother

Every good story has a beginning, a middle, and an end. But this beginning is a blur. The middle is missing, and I hope there is never an end.

Why am I writing this? The only thing I know is that what I feel for this man must be documented. It's a significant part of my memoir.

This man is more than a friend, but what is he? He is like, well, let's call him my blood brother.

My blood brother shares my soul. He understands me like few others. I would trust and have trusted him with my life.

This man, Roger, not only understands me, but he completely understands the relationship I had with Phil. He is the only one who fully understands, or so it seems to me.

Of all the cards I received after Phil's death, it is Roger's that I return to for solace. I return to his words over and over. He writes that he has always been envious of the loving relationship Phil and I had, that our sweetness and compatibility was unlike any couple he has ever known.

Roger is a deeply caring person. It is a rare thing to have a friend that listens, really listens to what you say, a friend who reflects upon your thoughts before responding.

One day he leaves a little gift of four cans of tomatoes under the wing of our airplane, that's sitting alone out on the flight line field, just because he knows we have no way to keep foods cold when we're airplane camping. A simple thing, really, but so touching.

He is a gentle man. He is intelligent. He is joyful and fun-loving. He lives life to the fullest and always.

This man is the one that takes all his friends' kids for a Stanley Park ride on the Christmas Eve Train, just for the joy of hearing those kids laughing. He's the one that builds them a swing that flies out over the ocean so they can drop into the depths. He's the one that buys a round of coffee and muffins for the airport manager's birthday.

He's the one that blasts his thundering airplane over our heads at Texada Island, coming out of nowhere, to shake and thrill us with a low-level pass, just for us, because he knows we're camping there. He pulls nearly straight up into the fluffy clouds. I can almost hear him chuckling.

This man never asks anything from anyone. He just wants to give.

This man makes the world a better place.

Roger had a long history as a pilot with Air Ontario but, now retired at a very young age, he flies for pleasure. And pleasure he gets!

We fly together to the Arlington Airshow in Washington.

Roger says, "Can we camp with you and Phil?"

He erects his tiny one-man tent, so small it fits just one sleeping bag, a little cocoon that zips an escape hatch only a few inches wide, it seems. Another friend puts up a tent, and so do we, but ours is to share! An intimate circle of teepees. It's a time of relaxation and great fun together while enjoying the airshow. In our camp, these two friends of ours proudly pound in and display their rainbow flag.

Phil says I love Roger because I feel safe with him. Although I don't know about that, I do know that he is a most special brother to me.

At home, ours is not a large airport, and there are always those who come to our airplanes to visit as we prepare for flight. Every one of them can be considered a friend, but none can compare to Roger. He is the most enthusiastic about flying and about us.

He is tall and extremely fit ~ a runner. Although he lives in a swanky Vancouver English Bay condo, his airplane is in a large, pristine hangar here, and yes, you can eat off the floors. Music is piped into this grand palace for an exquisite airplane.

He has the largest private plane here. The story of his acquisition of this plane began with a horror story.

Imagine this day. There are crowds of people, everyone milling about enjoying the local and visiting aircraft at the Qualicum Beach Airshow. Phil and I are standing nearby the hangars lining the flight line, just lazily soaking up the sun.

As we watch people and planes, Phil sees a disaster about to unfold. There is an airplane coming in to land, too close to the runway now. He has just performed multiple low passes, each with a steep climb out, an exciting thing for those there for a show! Its 1425-horsepower engine makes my heart flutter then pound. It is a large, powerful airplane, a Trojan T28, military trainer.

But then, as this colossal airplane is on the final approach, lower and lower, Phil shouts to me, "His landing gear is not down!"

Typical of Phil, he thinks of me first. He puts both his hands on my shoulders and says urgently, "Stay here!"

He turns quickly and runs fast, out from the crowd, and toward the runway. Phil flies an airplane with retractable gear as well and knows it will be a disaster to land without gear extended. Will the pilot and passenger survive this catastrophic event? Phil will be first on the scene because he knows the danger fully. He will be first to extract the pilot and passenger. He knows there is a danger of fire.

In the shadows of the hangar, I sob.

This is a bad thing to happen anywhere, but more so at a public airshow because the plane could easily swing off the runway into the crowd. The plane hits the runway with a terrible crash at a tremendously high speed. There is the sickening sound of metal screeching and the scraping of the airplane's belly on the runway as it slides. It slews sideways first one way then the other. The pilot has little control without the gear. How strange it looks on the ground and not up tall on its landing gear.

When it finally ceases to shriek and slithers sideways to a stop, I thank god there is no fire. The pilot and his passenger are pulled from the wreckage. They are not hurt, but they are in shock.

The plane did not make out so well. It is heartbreaking to see it loaded onto a trailer. It is to be hauled away for repair ~ if it even can be. This will be a very costly proposition, for a mangled propeller means an extensive engine reconstruction.

This plane is the that Roger purchases when the owner/pilot has to sell it after the expensive rebuild ~ the one Roger flies to this very day. He takes great pleasure in the throaty truculence of this beautiful aircraft, often thundering through with a low pass before landing.

He takes many excited individuals in the rear cockpit. And after every flight there a photo shoot and a little ceremony with Roger and each new passenger. They stand on the wing, everyone grinning, as he presents them with his standard gift. The plane is a Trojan, and so, what better gift than a condom?

There are historical events that have impacted my life in two ways. World Wars. My father trained as a gunner in World War II, which ended just before he flew combat.

And then, I flew with Phil in his World War II Harvard Trainer over five separate cenotaphs every November 11th Remembrance Day for 18 years. Phil dedicated himself to honouring those who gave their lives for the freedoms we have today.

We always fly in formation with Roger and with another friend, George, a former member of the famous Ray-Ban aerobatic team.

In the cozy airport coffee shop before our flypasts, we meet together every year on the November 11th morning. We are good friends. Over coffee, hands wrapped around our warm cups, we plan our strategy. It is a carefully choreographed flight with precision timing. We want to arrive at the Parksville cenotaph at ten seconds into the two minutes of silence. Planning is a wonderful time of camaraderie with good friends who must and do trust one another completely, flying in such tightly closed formation as we do. There is very little space between our wingtips. They are close, but they can never touch.

I hold this man Roger in high esteem partly because he is the one who honours Phil in the way I think Phil should be honoured. On November 2017, Roger put a three-column article in the local newspaper, full of the history of Phil initiating and continuing cenotaph flypasts since 1970, thereby honouring Phil greatly. Only Roger would do such a service for someone else. This man's heart is vast.

So, this November 11th, look up when you're at the cenotaph. Weather permitting, there will be a flypast. I will look down, and I will see you. We will remember the fallen and the serving together, you and I, for I have been invited to fly again, sharing camaraderie with, and taking great comfort from, this blood brother of mine.

Pilots keep flyover airborne

J.R. RARDON
jr.rardon@pqbnews.com

Airplane pilot Roger Yorke never flew for the Canadian military. But he knows a little something about military precision when it comes to the annual war plane flyover of Remembrance Day celebrations at Royal Canadian Legion branches across the mid-Island.

Yorke, a former Qualicum Beach resident, has flown his original 1955 T-28 Trojan military trainer over commemorations here for 17 years. He originally partnered with the late Phil Kalnin, who began the flyover in 1970 in his World War II-era Harvard fighter-trainer, and now teams with pilot George Kirbyson of Vancouver, a former member of the Ray Ban Gold Aerobatic Team who brings his own Harvard from the Canadian Museum of Flight in Langley.

"It's a very carefully choreographed and precisely timed event, to occur over the Parksville cenotaph at 10 seconds into the moment of silence," said Yorke, 56, who spent 13 years as a pilot for Air Ontario (now part of Jazz Aviation). "There is a miliary precision to ensure that timing.

"We want a solemn ceremony, we deem to be not too fast, not too slow, not too high and not too low."

The throaty, "truculent" sound of the planes' historic radial engines provides a nostalgic impact for older veterans on the ground, said Yorke, though he misses that impact while in the air.

"People, I'm told, react to it very favourably," Yorke said of the flyover. "It brings back memories. That is par-

> *I'm in a unique position to contribute to those who fought and died for those freedoms*
> **ROGER YORKE**

> 99

tially our goal, to honour those who sacrificed, but also to bring back those memories of service."

With its moment-of-silence flyover, Parksville is the signature location for what is actually a 45- to 50-minute flight that includes flyovers of Remembrance Day commemorations in Qualicum Beach, Bowser, Nanaimo, Ladysmith and Gabriola Island, said Yorke.

He said he and Kirbyson have tried to maintain the schedule established by Kalnin, who flew over each legion ceremony in the order in which he received the requests.

Yorke and Kirbyson will lift off from Qualicum Beach Airport, where Yorke's T-28 is hangared, at about 10:30 a.m. They will promptly fly over the Remembrance Day parade to the commemoration at the Qualicum Beach Civic Centre.

"Since Qualicum Beach has an enclosed ceremony, we fly over the parade so people get to see the aircraft in flight," Yorke said.

From there, it's on to Bowser, which will also be in the midst of its short parade to the Legion hall and its cenotaph commemoration.

The aviators will then "massage" their time over Parksville bay in order to arrive during the minute of silence in Parksville, Yorke said, then head south to perform flyovers of commemorations in Nanaimo, Ladysmith and Gabriola Island.

Yorke said he plans to continue the local flyovers as long as he is fit and able.

"Phil and I flew for a number of years together," said Yorke, who accepts no compensation for the flyover. "It's interesting, because Phil knew where to go. It requires local knowledge, and I'm uniquely situated to offer that.

"It is designed to be solemn because I take my liberties and freedoms very seriously. And I'm in a unique position to contribute to those who fought and died for those freedoms."

CHAPTER FORTY-FOUR

Once There Was

> Once there was
> There was
> And then
> There was not

One of the first lessons I learn in ground school is a goal ~ the goal of keeping the number of landings equal to the number of take-offs.

Sounds like a pretty good idea.

My passion for flying is a forever passion. I can't remember a time when I did not love airplanes. I hold my dad responsible for this, as I have vivid memories of him rounding us up when we are very young.

"Time to get ready for the airshow, kids!"

As if it is the most important thing. And, for me, it becomes almost the most important thing.

My love of airplanes never goes away.

Many years later, I have a friend, Jan, who is building his own airplane in his basement. The first time I see it, there is an entire wing mounted on the workshop wall. I stop in my tracks, stunned and enchanted.

This wing is stunning. This wing is like a spiritual beam of bright sunlight shining down on my soul, and I can't get the image of it out of my mind. I watch the aircraft progress month after month. One day there is a surprise.

"I will take you flying when it is finished," Jan says. And he does.

I am in the happiest place I have ever known when he lets me handle the plane. Then another surprise.

"That's all I will teach you for now," he says. "You need to sign up for flight school."

The very next morning, I do. That's all it takes ~ someone who has confidence in me.

"Sit in the pilot's seat," says the instructor. There are dual controls. He takes off from the passenger seat.

When we are at altitude, he says, "You have control."

Day one and I am given control! The concentration and intensity take me to a place I have not ever experienced before.

There is much to learn. I start with gaining altitude, losing altitude. I learn to reverse direction, and after completing a 360-degree turn, I am surprised when the instructor says, "Good. Feel that bump? That means you crossed the aircraft's own slipstream; you kept your altitude consistent."

I love the complexity and detail of everything I learn, and I race for my lesson every day after work.

And so it goes. Steadily.

One day while we're practicing take-offs and landings, the instructor says something a little unusual, "Taxi to the apron in front of the terminal, please."

As soon as I stop, he opens his door. He steps completely out of the airplane.

Standing on the tire, he says, "You're doing great. You're ready for your solo flight. Go!"

He shuts the door. He strides away, and he does not even look back. I begin to shake. I am alone in this airplane.

I self talk. "Are you going to be brave, or are you going to be a coward?"

"Charlie Foxtrot Echo X-Ray X-Ray, taxiing for runway 29."

I proceed to the button of the runway before I can't. And then I fly alone for the very first time. A small airplane is much lighter with only one soul aboard, and I feel terror regarding that empty seat beside me.

Then concentration takes over, and I am in control of both the aircraft and myself.

When I climb out of the airplane back at the flight school, I receive a hug from the instructor. Already I've forgiven him for his abandonment. I feel so many emotions. I laugh. I cry. I cry. I laugh.

The first cross-country trip is from Qualicum Beach direct to Victoria to land there and then return to Nanaimo so that I can refuel. Now I take off for Campbell River to land and then at last return to Qualicum Beach. As I near my home airport, a familiar voice calls in my headset. I've been gone for a long time.

My instructor jokes, "Oh, so you are going to return the plane, are you?"

Eventually, the flight test with the examiner is done and passed. The written tests are done and passed. At last and proudly, I hold my private pilot license.

My husband Phil wants me to learn to fly his very large and powerful WWII Harvard Warbird, but I tell him, "No, Phil! No, it is too much airplane for me as a beginner," so we look at airplanes for sale, and we settle on an ancient 1959 Piper for my very own. It is small. It is sort of like an airplane you put on ~ like a coat. We sit shoulder to shoulder, but we like it that way.

She is magnificent with wide pristine-white wings. I have a thing about wings. I love every inch of her. I wash and polish, grease and pamper her.

That little airplane takes us everywhere. We fly the island, the province, even Washington State for many, many years. We airplane-camp everywhere we go with our little pup tent nestled under the wing.

One of the places we love to fly to is Port Alberni. It's a gorgeous location in the forest. One day after a picnic lunch under the wing, we leave Port Alberni for the beautiful trip over the mountains toward home. I remember noticing the sunshine lighting the mountain range that day.

I am happily taking off for yet another wondrous flight when ~ there is a massive explosion

    Once there was

    There was

    An engine

    And then there was not

Instantly the cockpit fills with smoke. It is almost impossible to see. We are choking. Instinctively, my hand claws toward the window, but there is no time. I need to think clearly. Fly the airplane. Fly it at all times. Fly it with or, as it is now, without power.

I know I must not turn back to the runway at such a low altitude. Without thrust and lift, there is every chance the airplane's wings will stall, and we will spin.

There are only brief seconds for decision making. It has been drilled into my head that if ever there is an engine failure on takeoff, I must land straight ahead unless there is sufficient altitude, and right now, there is not sufficient altitude.

But straight ahead is a sea of stumps as far as I can see. We are too low. Those stumps are too close. Neither the airplane nor we would survive landing in that anyway.

Quickly, we decide to try to return to the runway. It is our only chance. I make the turn gradual, attempting to avoid a stall.

There is only eerie silence now. Terrifying silence. It's deafening.

Miraculously this little airplane stays airborne. She is gliding.

It is almost impossible to land an airplane without power adjustments, but in a few brief and very precious seconds, we touch down.

I brake hard, and Phil throws the door open for air. I turn off the magnetos and master switch, and we jump out quickly in case there is fire, but thank god, there is not. I attach the tow bar and hurry to tow the airplane clear of the runway because hot oil continues to pour out of the engine like lava.

We are both shaking uncontrollably. It is incomprehensible that this has actually happened.

We open the engine cowling now to see what went wrong, and we are shocked to see that the connecting rods have smashed again and again and again, completely through the engine crankcase.

Catastrophic injury. There are many gaping holes.

Maybe I did actually land this plane, but I like to think she landed herself. Though she is not a glider, she became one when she needed to. Our lives depended on it. A different airplane would never have pulled it off.

She had a Mt. Everest to climb that day, and she summited.

We pay homage to her and put in a new engine.

We give her life.

She certainly gave us ours.

CHAPTER FORTY-FIVE

My Most Recent Trip Around the Sun

In 2014 I am trying to survive my husband's death. His only wish is that I make myself happy. That's all he asks.

How am I doing this? Mostly, I'm not. And I'm looking for something that helps.

My husband Phil is not here to love me, to hug me, nor to laugh with me and tease me. But I will always remember that he tried so hard for three years so that he could stay a little longer with me.

I feel mired in loss. There's mud in my brain and in my heart.

Right away, my physician says I must go to go to Hospice.

I tell him I will – when I feel a little better.

He says that's precisely why I must go now.

Filled with grief, I step into that softly carpeted grand old Hospice House for the first time. Emotionally, it is almost unbearable, but I'm trying.

They tell me there that I will never be the same. But I already know that's true because how could I be?

Next, my doctor tells me that I could try to go to the gym.

I tell him I just can't do that right now, and then I do go because I am trying.

And, though I am trying, nothing seems to help.

These days I have an overwhelming desire to talk about Phil, to reminisce about his wonderful sense of humour, to remember his tender ways, to repeat his jokes. I speak to anyone and everyone who will listen.

My memories are of daring adventure with him. Memories of continuous laughter. Memories of conversations that never seem to end, and often last deep into the nighttime.

My memories are of fun, so much fun.

Phil's a believer. He believes everyone should be free to do what they want to do, not what someone else wants them to do and to be who they want to be. He accepts everyone; he believes in everyone.

Phil takes delight and pleasure in life, and all of it wonderfully amuses him. It's meant to be savoured. I have never known someone who treasures life as he does.

It's Phil's zest for life that makes his loss so devastating.

I feel like no one ever wants to live more than Phil does. I feel like few ever try so hard. He even somehow wrangles additional chemotherapy from the oncologists, though they have told us that nothing is going to work now.

His dying wish is that I make myself happy. That's all he asks. And I want to honour his request, but how can I do something so impossible?

For many years, I stumble through grief and my life. Mostly, I am numb.

When I decide that I want to write my memories of Phil, my memories of the "us" of us, I contemplate ideas, but I don't really know how to begin.

I am at home then a lot. I stay still, trying to cope, feeling not ready for the world as yet.

One day though, difficult as it is, I manage to get myself out the door. I stand in a line-up for tickets and have a conversation with someone who is also waiting. I happen to mention that I want to write about my husband.

Imagine my surprise when she tells me then that she teaches Memoir Writing. I am like a wide-eyed child in astonishment. We make introductions, exchange numbers.

This is a very timely conversation, and it brings to mind a Buddha quotation that goes something like, "When the student is ready, the teacher will appear."

Appear she did. An essential step in my survival begins that day. I glimpse a new horizon.

I feel like this may be something that helps.

I enroll in classes and learn a lot about writing. Then I pour the memories of our life together out of my heart and onto the pages. I learn, and I sweat, and eventually, I create an entire book of memoir which you now hold in your hands.

I am sitting at my old wooden desk one day, writing my memoir stories. My writing slows down. I lean back, and soon

I'm dreaming of Phil's wonderful sense of humour that I miss so much. My favourite Phil-joke wiggles itself into my mind to make me laugh. I'd like to share it.

Phil says there are two little boy vampire bats just hanging about in the cave.

One says to the other, "I am going out to get me some blood."

He returns with blood dripping from his face.

His friend says, "Wow, where'd you get the blood?"

The first bat points.

"Can you see that telephone pole over there?"

"Yeah," says the friend.

"Well, I didn't."

It's a pretty good joke on its own – poor little bat running into the telephone pole.

But the best part is that our friend who is listening one day tells Phil just a little sarcastically that bats don't need to see.

"Phil, they use echolocation."

"They don't talk either," says Phil. "It's a joke."

During the last year, my most recent trip around the sun, I learn that my writing teacher is a storyteller. I attend every storytelling show she is in. I become fascinated, so we change my class. My writing classes now become Storytelling 101. How very exciting this new life is. I listen carefully. I accept critique willingly because I want to become a good storyteller.

It is a struggle to remember what I want to say in the stories I tell, and it is a process, but eventually, I begin to have just a minute flicker of confidence.

In this, the later part of my life, there is not much I am afraid of anymore, but my knees shake and my voice trembles when I step behind the microphone in front of an audience to tell a story the very first time. The terror I feel at that moment would have stopped me before Phil, but he has changed me, and I feel his presence and forge on.

This first venue is blessedly small, only thirty people. At the beginning of the first story I tell, I miss a vital part of the story, and when I realize it ~ thank god, I did realize it ~ I have to think quickly on my feet to fit that important part somehow back in so the story makes sense. I am so surprised that I manage to do that and greatly relieved when it works.

The next show is much larger, and I find I am unable to mingle with my friends ahead of telling. I closet myself away in another room in seclusion, just trying to remember the confounded first three words of my story, let alone all of it.

Nothing much helped in my grief recovery before, but storytelling for me is life-altering. Slowly, I am finding my way again ~ through much remembering and writing but exceedingly through Storytelling. It has transformed my life.

I have not moved on. But I have moved forward ~ with him. I am doing this by myself and for myself. I feel strength, courage, even hope. I have a joyous feeling around me. It feels a little like ~ well, it feels like ~ oh look, the sun coming out again ~

I am, at last, honouring Phil's request that I make myself happy.

But there's just one little thing I'd love to know.

Are you listening, Phil?

Are you smiling?

Oh, yes, I know you are.

CHAPTER FORTY-SIX

Hands

There is nothing so welcome as when someone takes my hand.

In my life, there have been hands leading me toward danger and hands leading me away from it.

I have taken hands, and I have had mine taken.

When I am little, my father holds my hand to tell me my friend has been killed. I will never see her again.

I've given my hand marriage. Twice. Once a mistake. One time to the love of my life.

I've taken the hand of a child ~ my child.

I have leant a hand to those in need. I've given a hand up.

I have given away hand-me-downs and worn them, too.

I've been a handful and raised a handful.

I've raised a hand and kept it down, too, afraid to speak up.

I've clapped my hands and waved them eagerly.

One day a man asked for my hand in marriage.

On the most intimate, romantic, enchanting, and happiest day of my life, I gave my hand ~ gave it, along with my heart. This man took my hand in adventure and captivation. This man taught me much. Taught me about love and laughter and about not taking things so seriously.

But then serious does come to us. He is diagnosed with cancer. He takes my hand in fear. I give my hand in comfort.

We walk hand-in-hand through chemo, but life deals us a cruel hand.

When family comes, this man holds up his hands and says, "There will be no sorrow. I want to hear laughter."

My hands care for this man. I keep him at home. My hands take care of his every need.

When he takes his last breath, my hands take his hands, while my soul screams, "No!"

This man made no complaint and made only one request ~ that I make myself happy.

To honour him, these hands have tried to do that, as hard as it is. These hands have kept busy with family, friends, and trying to figure out how to go on.

Now I'm reading what these hands have written.

I am perhaps making progress. And yet, these hands have wiped tears for years.

ACKNOWLEDGMENTS

It is impossible to fully express my gratitude to my friends, Gloria and Jeff Carpenter. From the beginning, you have listened to endless stories and have unfailingly offered the best, most thoughtful critique. Jeff, your vast writing experience has proved invaluable. Your abiding enthusiasm and continuous interest has provided me with immeasurable and greatly appreciated encouragement.

Marva Blackmore, my teacher, my editor, my friend. Where would I be without you? Everything wonderful, I've learned from you, and the process has been a great joy. It is incredible to me how you hear every story-word and how you recognize my intent, then offer your wisdom. I am grateful beyond words. I will never forget the incredible coincidence that we even met.

ABOUT THE AUTHOR

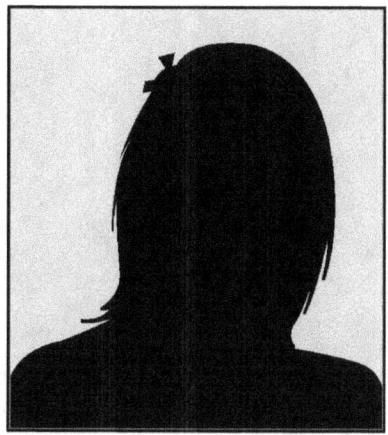

Lee Kalnin knows a thing or two about grief, having lost her husband in 2014. His shared memories are described here, along with her own. A great deal of their lives had centered around a passion for flying and the resulting high adventure.

Lee's more recent passion is for Storytelling for Adults, which is reflected in this memoir.

She lives in Parksville, British Columbia, Canada.

This is her first book.

www.ingramcontent.com/pod-product-compliance
Lightning Source LLC
Chambersburg PA
CBHW070421010526
44118CB00014B/1857